NO ONE
CRIES THE
WRONG WAY

Seeing God Through Tears

REFLECTIONS ON

The Goodness of God and the Mystery of Human Suffering

Dying Well

Life After Death

Grieving

Caring for People in Loss

Prayer in Tough Times

FATHER JOE KEMPF

Our Sunday Visitor Publishing Division
Our Sunday Visitor, Inc.
Huntington, Indiana 46750

Nihil Obstat
Rev. Dennis J. Colter

Imprimatur
✠ Most Rev. Jerome Hanus OSB
Archbishop of Dubuque
September 19, 2001

Copyright © 2012 Fr. Joseph Kempf
Published 2012 by Our Sunday Visitor.

Big Al ™ Fr. Joseph Kempf

17 16 15 14 13 12   1 2 3 4 5 6 7 8 9
ISBN: 978-1-61278-602-5
LCCN: 2012930241

Our Sunday Visitor Publishing Division
Our Sunday, Visitor, Inc.
200 Noll Plaza
Huntington, IN 46750

1-800-348-2440
bookpermissions@osv.com

PRINTED IN THE UNITED STATES OF AMERICA

CONTENTS

INTRODUCTION VI

PART ONE

CHAPTER ONE

The Question 2

Misunderstanding the Causes of Suffering 4
Why Do We Suffer?.. 7
Why Doesn't God Stop All Suffering? 9
Yes, but 9

CHAPTER TWO

The Answerer 11

The Face of God 12
I Will Go with You....................................... 14

CHAPTER THREE

The More Important Question 16

Who Hides in You? 18
Humble Birthing 19
Glimpses.. 20
Leaping into Darkness 20

CHAPTER FOUR

Why Pray? 22

Words 23
What Happens When We Pray? 24
What about Miracles? 25
A Greater Good 27
Like Little Children..................................... 28

PART TWO

CHAPTER FIVE

Dignity in Life and in Death 30

Facing Our Own Death 32
End-of-Life Medical Care 34
Dying Well 35
Facing the Death of One We Love 35
Tangible Presence 37
Solidarity 38

CHAPTER SIX

The Birth that Is Death—Life after Life 40

Death Does Not End a Relationship 42

CHAPTER SEVEN

To Grieve 44

No One Cries the Wrong Way 45
Common Grief Reactions 46
Complicating Grief 50
Our Role in the Grief Process 51
Letting Ourselves Receive 53
Children Grieve, Too 54
Helps for Children 56

CHAPTER EIGHT

We Are God's Response 58

"Putting Skin On" God 59
Presence 60
What Do We Say? The Danger of Words .61
The Gift of a Small Kindness 63

PART THREE

INTRODUCTION

Chapter One Prayer Service 67

Chapter Two Prayer Service 71

Chapter Three Prayer Service 75

Chapter Four Prayer Service 79

Chapter Five Prayer Service 83

Chapter Six Prayer Service 87

Chapter Seven Prayer Service 91

Chapter Eight Prayer Service 95

Face-to-Face with Jesus—A Guided Meditation 100

INTRODUCTION

It was my sophomore year in college when the questions first became real for me. My friend Vivian collapsed during play practice, and died several days later without ever regaining consciousness. Through the blur of my own tears, I watched Vivian's family stagger through those days, racked with pain. Suddenly, I wondered about God. Did God know this was going to happen? Was this God's idea? Did God have anything to do with this at all?

After Vivian's death I began to read whatever I could find that might help me understand, including works of great scholars and theologians. I talked to my classmates, my seminary professors, and everyone I thought might have something worthwhile to say, because, in my grief, the questions were so important to me. Now, after 21 years of priesthood, the questions are just as real for me—and even more important.

As people of faith we are invited to trust in the wonderful goodness of God. Then how are we to understand the sufferings of so many of God's people? Where is God to be found in the midst of a world filled with so much loss and pain? How do we respond to someone who asks why God allowed his or her child to die? What difference does it make to pray? What is our hope when we stand at the bedside of a loved one who is dying?

This book offers some simple glimpses into these great questions. At the end of the book, there is a prayer service for each chapter, questions for reflection or discussion, and quotes for meditation and prayer. I encourage you to stop after each chapter and spend time with this material to help you wrestle with the questions.

Certainly, there are no easy answers. Any words about God will ultimately fall far short of the truth of who God is. Indeed, we stand here before great mystery. But we do not stand alone; without hope; or without something to offer.

My own struggle to understand the suffering of God's people continues to lead me ever more deeply to the humble beauty of God. The God who, in Jesus, embraces our every suffering, and who births life from what we know as death.

I think it is extremely important that we wrestle with the questions. For in the end, they lead us to love.

PART ONE

History is not fixed. It does not move inevitably towards either perfection or destruction . . . history has a capacity for being changed from within.

—Douglas John Hall

THE QUESTION

*"There is always a night-shift, and sooner
or later we all are put on it."*
—Evelyn Underhill

Though it has only three letters, no word has borne more pain. Sometimes this word has been shouted in anger; sometimes it has been whispered through tears that seem to never end. It rises in our chests as we sit with the news of a tragic loss; it grasps us by the throats as we weep at the graveside of one who died too soon. The all too familiar word is *"Why?"* Why did she have to die? Why not me? Why didn't I know?. . . Why . . . Why . . . Why . . . The countless "whys" turn like a fishhook in our hearts.

For people of faith, that word strikes at our very understanding of God. Certainly, there are many Scriptures that describe a God of great compassion and love:

"Can a mother forget her infant, be without tenderness for the child of her womb? Even should she forget, I will never forget you." *(Isaiah 49:15)*

"I have called you by name, and you are mine." *(Isaiah 43:1)*

"And know that I am with you always, until the end of the world." *(Matthew 28:20)*

Yet, often in the face of the enormity of human suffering, we wonder.

In the beginning of his book *The Road Less Traveled,* M. Scott Peck summarizes all of life with these three words: "Life is difficult." We would like to think that life should *not* be difficult or painful, but it is. There is indeed a tragic element to human life, and no one escapes suffering.

Once a pre-kindergarten teacher found a fun activity for her class. She wrote a song about popcorn, taught it to her students, and then had them crouch down on the floor to sing it. At the appropriate point in the song, all the children would "pop up," and soon the teacher had them popping all over the classroom. One day, the popcorn song was in full swing when the teacher noticed one little boy who remained crouching on the floor while the other children "popped" all over the room. "What's wrong?" the teacher asked, "Why aren't you popping like the other children?" The little boy replied, "I'm burning on the bottom of the pan."

We all have days like that: times when the ordinary frustrations and struggles of daily living make us feel like we too are "burning on the bottom of the pan." Yet sometimes, when we experience a tragedy or loss and the pain seems almost unbearable, we yearn for those days that merely annoyed us, when it seemed that we were simply burning on the bottom of the pan.

For every one of the Scriptures that tenderly describes a loving God, there are countless examples of tragedy and loss: A drunken driver kills the parents of small children; an aged woman watches helplessly as mental illness robs her of her husband; a little boy is stricken with cancer; thousands of children starve to death each day; a young girl is raped; a hurricane rips through an impoverished village; political prisoners are brutally tortured; a couple with very little money gives birth to a child with severe birth defects. And the list goes on and on—a list that grows longer with the addition of *our own* stories of pain and loss. And then that question arises again, the word that catches in our throats, wrenches our stomachs, flows through our tears: *Why?*

In the face of suffering, some choose to believe that there must not be a God— that there simply *cannot* be a God. How could there be a God in the face of such pain? What kind of God would allow such things? Doesn't God see? Doesn't God care? What difference did it make that we prayed? Where is God now?

It is important that we use great care in our thinking when facing these great mysteries.

Misunderstanding the Causes of Suffering

Regarding the causes of suffering, three of the most common errors suggest that God, for various reasons, is the one who sends us suffering.

Misunderstanding #1

The first mistake is to think that God causes us to suffer because God doesn't want us to be too happy. In this mindset, life is meant by God to be a "vale of tears," and if we want to be happy in the *next* life, we must be unhappy in *this* life.

Columnist Erma Bombeck once wrote about a child she observed in church on a Sunday morning. The child, sitting in the pew in front of Erma, was happily looking around and smiling at other churchgoers. The child was not tearing up the hymnal, throwing things out of its mother's purse, or creating any other form of havoc. The child was simply smiling. When the child's mother saw this, she leaned over, swatted the child on the backside and scolded, "Stop smiling, you're in church!" And, as a tear trickled down the little child's face, the mother whispered, "That's better," and returned to her prayers.

One of the great wisdoms of our Church is knowing that this is *not* how God is. Just as loving parents delight to see their children happy, so does God want fullness of life for us. As the Book of Wisdom says, "God did not make death" *(1:13)*. Instead, as Jesus says of himself, "I came so that they might have life and have it more abundantly" *(John 10:10)*.

Misunderstanding #2

The second mistake is to think that God causes suffering to punish us for our sins. Even if we would not normally think like this, when tragedy strikes, it is common that we find ourselves wondering if God might not be "getting back at us" for our sins. How many people have wondered such things as: "If we had been going to church every Sunday, maybe we would never have been in that accident," or "Perhaps our child died because God was punishing us for having sex before we got married?" Once again, the Church's wisdom teaches us we do *not* have a God like that.

When we choose sin, *we* are choosing that which does not give life. Sin by its very nature hurts us and others. When we choose sin, we choose the harm that is the consequence of that sin. The choice of sin is the choice of the *death* that sin is. God is not somewhere "out there" waiting to inflict suffering on us or on our loved ones as punishment for our sins.

The Book of Job powerfully teaches us that we do not have a God who is waiting to punish us because of our sins. Some of the religious leaders of Job's day tried to convince him that his sufferings were because God was punishing him for some sin he must have committed. Job was familiar with this type of thinking, and he knew that there was some truth to the argument that there is a blessing for good living, and there is unhappiness for foolish and evil conduct. But Job also came to know that some tragedies just happened in life and were not inflicted by God as punishment for sin.

Jesus also disagreed with those religious leaders of his day who taught that suffering was a consequence of sin. Once, when the disciples came upon a man who had been born blind, they asked Jesus whether his blindness was caused by the blind man's sin or by the sin of his parents. Jesus told them that his suffering was not the consequence of any sin *(John 9:3)*. We do not have a God who sends suffering to punish us for our wrongdoing, but a God who again and again *forgives* our sin, loving us beyond what we can imagine—even *as* we sin!

Misunderstanding #3

The third, and probably most common, mistake about the origin of human suffering is often heard in clichés at funeral homes, churches, and whenever the discussion turns to someone's misfortune or loss. The third misunderstanding again names God as the cause of our suffering, but this time for some higher purpose—to bring good out of our pain.

Most of us have heard this in one form or another. When tragedy strikes, or people are confronted with loss, many people say things like: "God never gives us more than we can handle," or "God never closes a door without opening a window." Or perhaps we hear the phrase: "Everything happens for a reason," which seems to suggest that God has intentionally caused suffering for some higher purpose. We are told that "It is God's will, we just don't understand yet why God did this." Some suggest that God is testing our faith or making us grow. Each of these attitudes implies that God's perfect ways are not our ways. Though we will probably never understand now, in heaven we will understand why God did all this.

For many, there is some initial comfort in this type of thinking. At a time when the ground beneath our feet is shaking, we are often ready to grab onto anything that might provide some security. Yet, we need to think carefully about such clichés. Are they actually true? Does saying that everything happens for a reason mean God intentionally caused this suffering for some other reason? If "God never gives us more than we can handle," does that mean God gave me this tragedy? What kind of God would that be? Even though we have heard these thoughts many times, that does not make them true.

Some years ago on Christmas Day, my friend Jean rushed her daughter Terri to the hospital. Days earlier, Terri had bubbled with the same excitement that most ten-year-old children do in anticipation of Christmas. But she woke up on Christmas Eve not feeling right, and soon was struggling for her life. In the end, she would lose that battle, dying several days later without ever having opened her Christmas presents. I stood next to Jean at the funeral home as caring people, in an attempt to be consoling, said things to her like: "I'm sure that God did this for a better purpose," or "I'm sure that God had a very good reason for taking Terri's life." Later she would turn to me and say, "I'm supposed to pray to a God who would take my daughter's life for a better reason? What reason would be good enough? I do not believe that God caused this."

Nor do I.

Yes, we believe that God is indeed a part of every moment in each of our lives. Indeed, it is often in suffering—as in no other place —that God's goodness can birth a new good in us. Often, when we look back on a particular suffering, we can see the beautiful ways that God's loving presence sustained us and brought us to a deeper life. But it is flawed logic to think simplistically that, since God wants me to grow, and since I have grown through suffering, then God must have sent the suffering to me so that I could grow.

Our faith tells us that God is intricately woven into the fabric of our every moment and that nothing can happen outside of the providence of God. That does not mean that our sufferings themselves are something that God caused. But in the end we believe that no matter what our suffering, God can bring good out of it in ways that surpass our understanding in this life.

Why Do We Suffer?

Where do our sufferings come from?

Human Sin

Clearly, much of the suffering of the world comes directly as the result of sinful human choices. Sometimes it is easy to see that a particular suffering is not God's idea but is born from human sin. We know that it is not "God's will" that a child be abused, a person raped, or anyone murdered, but it is rather the result of human weakness and sin. Though countless wars and other acts of violence have been done "in the name of God," in such instances, God's name has been taken in vain, for clearly such hatred is not God's will.

Institutionalized Evil

There are other tragedies that are the result of sin, too, but in less obvious ways. That thousands of people starve to death daily is less a result of conscious intention and more the result of an "institutionalized" greed. Like the rich man in Luke's Gospel *(16:19–31)* who did not see the beggar who was at his feet longing to eat the scraps that fell from the table, we often fail to see those who are hungry in the world or recognize our deep inter-connection with all God's creatures. Sometimes, we are so narrow and individualistic in our descriptions of sin that we fail to see the tremendous suffering caused by the arms race or by our economic decisions that hurt those who are poor.

For example, though I deplore the damage that is being done to the environment and the daily extinction of many species of plant and animal life, it is something for which I bear some responsibility by my own use of this world's goods. There is an evil in the world that is greater than each of us, but it is also part of us. We all bear some responsibility for the starvation of God's children, the racism that keeps so many oppressed, and the ravaging devastation of our planet. Such sufferings, too, are clearly not God's will.

Ego

Certainly, some of our pain is self-inflicted. Sometimes we suffer, or inflict suffering on others, because we cling too tightly to our own egos. It is usually without even realizing it that we become over-identified with our own agendas, successes, failures, or desires. We cause great suffering in the world by our need to be successful, to be certain, and especially, by our need to be *right*. How difficult it is to let go.

The story is told of researchers who needed to capture a certain species of monkey for experimentation. They placed some nuts inside long, narrow-necked jars and left these jars at various locations on the jungle floor. The monkeys, drawn by the smell of the nuts, reached their hands into the jar and grabbed a fistful of the nuts. When they tried to pull their hands back out, the fists they made with the nuts were now too big to fit through the neck of the jars. However, the monkeys would not let go. Rather than let the nuts go and slide their hands back out, they stubbornly held onto the nuts with their arms stuck in the jars and chattered angrily until the researchers came and simply tossed a net over them.

As unflattering as the comparison might be, I fear that we are often like those monkeys. How desperately we cling to our wants, our desire to control things, our self-image, our plans, and even our image of God. We often cling tightly to our egos instead of doing the painful, but necessary, work of letting go into transformation.

Lack of Forgiveness

Being unforgiving has been described as drinking rat poison, and then waiting for the rat to die. How many of us carry inside ourselves the poison of a grudge, a lack of forgiveness? Though Jesus was clear about the absolute necessity of forgiving, this is a hard lesson for us to learn. We derive a certain gratification from thinking angry thoughts about, or even wishing evil on, those who have wronged us. By this, we sometimes do hurt those against whom we bear a grudge. However, in not forgiving, we also destroy ourselves.

These are some of the sufferings caused—not by God—but by ourselves. There are many others. Certainly, we humans are, by far, the greatest cause of suffering in the world.

Why Doesn't God Stop All Suffering?

Since so much of the suffering of the world is the exact opposite of what God wants, some wonder why God allows—and does not stop—evil. The truth is *God is radically committed to our free will* and will not force us to be loving or just. What is God to do: grab the steering wheel from a drunken driver, or stay our hands when we intend to inflict suffering on one another? God who is "all powerful" has chosen a *"powerlessness"* before our freedom. Though God is always calling us—and empowering us—to act with love and justice, God will never force us to live in any certain way.

We sometimes hear the phrase "God's will" used as if everything that happened were somehow part of a pre-ordained plan in which human freedom played no role. What if we were to understand "God's will" as an invitation to love no matter what the situation that we find ourselves in?

Yet that invitation comes with no certainty that we will respond well.

By naming God as the cause of all suffering, people may be tempted to avoid confronting the enormity of human responsibility for the sufferings of the world. Indeed, in most cases, the answer to the question "Why?" points to us.

In what Jesus taught, and in how Jesus lived, we see clearly that God yearns for an end to all the suffering we inflict on one another. God is always calling us to a greater love, and in that call comes the power of love in order that we might be transformed. But God will never force us — that's not what love does.

Yes, but . . .

But what of the other sufferings not caused by our sinfulness? What about the death of innocent children to diseases or the suffering caused by accidents or natural disasters? How can we understand these?

We know that the poisoning of our environment, and the hatred and selfishness we pass down from generation-to-generation do affect the amount of illness in the world. However, in the end, there is no satisfactory rational explanation to the question "why" in the face of the sufferings caused by disease and accidents. God is wonderfully alive in the world for us at every moment. Yet, our very human nature is frail and full of suffering. Though it might seem as very little comfort to someone in the midst of great loss, suffering is intrinsic to the very nature of our human frailty. Suffering, while not outside the providence of God, is not something that God inflicts on us. Illness, injury, death, and accidents are all a part of our limited, frail human condition.

Perhaps God could have made us robots, dictating our every step. Had God done this, there would have been no suffering, no tears, and no death. But there would have also been no love, for there is only love when there is freedom *not* to love. Clearly, God wanted us to have a heart like God's own. Instead of creating us as robots, God created us with the ability to love. In this, God gave us the capacity for the other suffering, the great suffering that is at the center of God's own heart: the freely chosen suffering of love.

Sometimes, I picture God at the time of our birth holding us gently, looking at us with deepest tenderness, and whispering, "My precious child, I love you more than you could ever know. So much do I love you that I want you to be like me. And so, I set you free—free to love, free to serve, free to laugh and dance, free to cry. Yes, even free to suffer. For I give you a heart like my heart. Go now to love the world."

And, like God, we cannot stop every evil or protect everyone from harm. But, as we shall see, in our fight against what is evil in the world, in our readiness to stand in solidarity with those who are marginalized, in our willingness to walk side-by-side, and even weep, with those in pain, we are more like God than at any other time. For that is exactly how God loves. In this we will meet the final cause of our suffering—we suffer because we have a heart like God's own.

> *"There is always a night-shift, and sooner or later we all are put on it."*
> —Evelyn Underhill

THE ANSWERER

"Until you have cried, you do not know God."

—Saint Ephraem

Because it was Christmas Eve, there was an unofficial cease-fire on the battlefield. Floodlights eerily lit up the area between the opposing armies. One of the allied soldiers, a member of the Royal Argyle Sutherland Highlanders, described what happened that night in the loneliness of being at war and far away from home.

He said that as he and his fellow soldiers sat in their trenches, tired, scared, and lonely, they heard music from across the battlefield. Though they did not understand the words, they recognized the melody. They realized that they were hearing the song "Silent Night" being sung by the German soldiers in their native tongue. This young soldier noticed that several of his fellow soldiers had begun to sing along in English, and he himself soon joined in. He said the most amazing thing happened then. Still singing, soldiers from the opposing trenches got up and began to walk toward one another on the battlefield.

As the enemy soldiers drew near to one another, the young allied soldier found himself standing opposite a young German soldier. The German soldier reached into his pocket, pulled out a small flask of cognac, took a quick drink, and then held it out offering it to him. He hesitated, then accepted the gesture, and took a drink. The allied soldier reached into his pocket to find something to offer back but only found half a candy bar. He held it out to the young German soldier who took it and smiled. At that moment, the two soldiers looked into each other's eyes. As they did so, something inside them melted, and they saw what was most true. In that moment, they realized that they were more alike than different. They were both homesick and scared, more brothers than they were enemies. They threw their arms around each other and cried. Standing in the middle of the battlefield, they sobbed in each other's arms.

When those soldiers looked into each other's eyes, they saw more than the enemy they expected to see. By looking into each other's eyes, they saw the deeper truth of who they were, a truth they would have never known without that look.

Something similar happens to us when we look into the face of suffering. In the face of suffering, we can find something of the humble beauty of God.

The Face of God

There is a tendency to think that God must be somehow distant from our suffering. If God does not will our pain, then God must at least pull away in horror and choose to be somewhere else more fittingly majestic. Yet, the very opposite is true. God has made a home in suffering. Unless we look into the face of pain and sorrow, there is something of God that we will never know.

One of the great weaknesses of our culture is our tendency to turn our faces away and to deny the reality of human suffering, except for those times when it touches our own lives in a way we can't avoid. There is a pervasive tendency to escape by numbing ourselves with TV or alcohol. We sometimes turn to buying things, to being extremely busy, or to mouthing religious clichés, all done to avoid seeing the reality of human pain. However, we do this at peril to our souls. Though we might be tempted to turn our heads away—unless we are willing to see the great suffering of the world—there is something of the beauty of God's face that we will never see.

The Answerer

Shortly before I was ordained a priest, my classmates and I were challenged by our retreat master to "tithe our time with the poor." He told us how important it was that we spend time with those who wear their brokenness on the outside: persons with disabilities; those who are hungry, grieving, or imprisoned; and all those who are so often quickly dismissed by society. He told us that in doing so, we would see the truth of our own brokenness, and realize our deep solidarity with all those who suffer. He also told us that there we would meet the God who comes in powerlessness. He told us that, if we did not meet God there, we might never meet God. I think he was right.

Though not easily recognized by those who suffer, God is present in the midst of our suffering in a way that is more humble and beautiful than we could ever imagine. It is not, however, a presence that necessarily gives answers or makes everything okay.

One of the deepest yearnings of every human heart is for relationship with God. When Job cried out "Why?" in the midst of his sufferings, God's response did not give Job answers that explained away the mystery of human suffering. But God did offer Job what humans most deeply yearn for: God gave him relationship. God spoke to him, and in this, Job was given the opening to see that his God had not abandoned him.

As we, like Job, face the mystery of our suffering, we are called to trust that we are not alone, for our God is in it with us!

This is, for Christians, the true meaning of the cross. The cross stands forever for us as the most powerful statement of the love of God: the God who will never abandon us; the God who has, in Jesus, embraced our every human suffering.

Some years ago, I was blessed to experience a thirty-day retreat. In one exercise, I was asked to sit with the Scriptures about Jesus' death, and, in my imagination, picture myself there. The crucifixion was for me a vividly ugly scene. I saw Jesus on the cross, his face blotted with blood and spit, his body racked with pain.

I turned away, and sat overwhelmed in the deafening silence. Then I heard a sound and realized it was the sound of someone crying. When I turned and looked, I saw that it was Jesus weeping on the cross. I wanted to turn away. Seeing Jesus weeping on the cross wrenched my heart because then I knew that *Jesus knew* how bad it was. He didn't simply go through the motions of some great drama, untouched by the reality of the pain. His dream was shattered. He was mocked, beaten, spat upon, racked with pain, and he knew it! He felt utterly alone in his pain. He was weeping.

The image of Jesus weeping on the cross changed forever my knowing of God. I could never again think that God was "aloof" or distant from human pain. Not only does God understand what it is like for us to suffer; the "all powerful" God has actually chosen, in Jesus, to suffer *with us*.

That, in part, is why it is so important that we look at the face of suffering. In suffering, as in no other place, we see something of the astounding beauty of God's love. In Jesus, we see the God of self-emptying love who has chosen to embrace our every pain; to suffer what we suffer; and even to die with us. Many times as I have been with people who are grieving or suffering, and who wondered where God was, I've sensed that God was right there, weeping with them! Though there is a great loneliness in suffering, we never suffer alone.

Any response to the questions of the sufferings of the world must include the humility of a God who has entered into our every pain and loss, the God who suffers with us. As we will look at in the next section, by embracing our every suffering, God can transform our loss to a new good. Here, as people of faith, we will again meet paradox: the unbelievable love of a God who is both *beyond* us and yet *with* us in our suffering.

I Will Go With You

The humble beauty of the presence of God with us in our suffering is illustrated for me by Solomon Rosenberg's story of his family's experience in one of the Nazi death camps. This particular camp was a work camp—as long as a person could work they could escape the gas chambers. In the family of Solomon Rosenberg, the first to go were his aged parents who were well into their 80s, and who broke quickly under the inhuman conditions.

Solomon knew that the next to go in his family would probably be their younger son David, who was slightly physically disabled, and was able now to work less and less. Each morning the family would be separated for their work assignments, and each night when they came back to huddle together in the barracks the father returned frightened—wondering whether this might be the day that David would be taken. Each night as he entered the barracks, his eyes quickly sought out his little boy David, his oldest boy Jacob, and his wife, the mother of his children.

Then came the night that he feared. As he walked into the barracks, he could see none of his family and became frantic. His eyes searched again for the precious faces of his family members. Finally, he saw the figure of his oldest boy Jacob, hunched over and weeping in the corner. He still could not see David or his wife. He hurried to Jacob and said, "Son, tell me it isn't so. Did they take David today?" "Yes, Papa," he said through his tears, "today they came to take David. They said he could no longer do his work."

And Solomon could feel his heart break.

"But Mama, where is Mama? She still is strong. Surely, they wouldn't take Mama, too?"

Jacob looked at his father through his tears and said, "Papa, Papa. When they came to take David, he was afraid, and he cried. So Mama said to David, 'You don't have to be afraid, David. I will go with you and hold you close.'"

And she did just that. Jacob's mother went with her son to the gas chamber, holding him close so he wouldn't have to be afraid.

I am convinced that, together, they were held by God. For that is the kind of God we have—one who does not cause our suffering, but rather embraces it with us.

At the very end of Matthew's Gospel, Jesus said, "And know that, I am with you always, until the end of the world." There is no place we can go, no situation we could ever find ourselves in, that God is not already there filled with love for us, embracing our sufferings, weeping with us, and holding us close.

> *"Until you have cried, you do*
> *not know God."*
> —Saint Ephraem

THE MORE IMPORTANT QUESTION

"Faith is the bird that feels the light and sings when the dawn is still dark."

—Rabindranath Tagore

Several years ago, a young woman named Michelle moved into the parish where I was assigned. Michelle was full of life and energy, and anxious to be a part of the parish community. She also was suffering from occasional flare-ups of the disease, Lupus. At the age of 24, she went in for surgery to lessen the inflammation in her back and came out instead paralyzed for life. The news was crushing.

Our parish family joined Michelle's biological family, and prayed with her, cried with her, laughed with her, and tried to sustain her with our hope and faith. We were saddened that we could not make everything okay, but loved her in the midst of it all the best that we could.

Several years after the onset of her paralysis, I asked Michelle the question, "If there was such a thing as a 'magic pill' that would bring you back completely to the way you were before the accident, not just physically, but also emotionally, spiritually, relationally, would you take it?" Michelle thought about that a while and said, "At first, I think that, if there were such a pill, I probably would have taken it. I'd have loved to walk and run and ski again. Now, I realize how much more alive I am because of what I've suffered. My eyes are open wider, and I realize, more than ever before, what truly matters. If that pill brought me back to how I was before, physically, and in all ways, would I take it?" She looked at me from her wheelchair and said quietly, "No, I would not."

Michelle is not the only one to say that. I have talked with many who faced unwanted difficulty or tragedy, who are now more alive than ever because of what God was able to bring forth *from the suffering*. They don't blame God for their suffering, but they found that God was with them in ways that brought them life from what seemed like only death. God brought them to a new life, one that they could not have found except through what they suffered.

This, however, does not deny the reality of loss and pain. Sometimes our whole world is changed in a moment. Perhaps it is by a call from the police department telling us to come to the hospital. Maybe it is a shocking news report of great tragedy or terror, or maybe it is through the note left on the counter telling us "goodbye," that the relationship is over. Or maybe it is the look in the doctor's eyes when he says, "I'm sorry . . . ." The traumatic news can come in countless ways, but when it does, it can leave us feeling as if our entire world has been shattered. Life is suddenly and forever different, and we wonder how we could ever go on—or why we would even want to.

Such was the death of Jesus. As Jesus surrendered himself to the cross, his body was broken, his blood poured out, and the silence was deafening.

Yet, as he faced his death, Jesus clung to the promise of his Father to bring life out of his death. The good news, the wonderful news, is that the God who reigns even over suffering, did just that. Were it to have ended for Jesus with his death, as Saint Paul says, "your faith is in vain" *(1 Corinthians15:17)*.

But it did not end there. The silence of Good Friday yielded to the beautiful song of Easter. That is *our* hope. For the promise is, that what God did for Jesus, God will do for us, Christ's body.

Christ has died, Christ is risen, Christ will come again. That is *the* pattern, *the* story: every dying done in love leads to life. It was the pattern for Jesus, and it is the pattern for all who would ever follow his way. In the cross, we see that there is nothing we suffer that God has not already embraced. In the resurrection, we see that even the most unspeakable tragedy cannot destroy us.

God's promise is not to free us from all pain or loss, but to redeem our suffering with a new good wrought by love. We can trust that, though evil and sin are real and painful, they are not decisive. Though there is an essentially tragic element to human life, love is ultimately victorious. Such is the incredible beauty of God.

Who Hides in You?

A woman who had done missionary work in Alaska described the work of the Avilik ivory carvers. Before they ever touched a knife to the ivory, these carvers would gently hold the raw fragment, slowly turning it this way and that. Then they would whisper to the ivory, "Who are you? Who hides in you?" They were convinced that the forms of animals, people, or various things to carve were contained within. Rather than force their will onto the ivory, they wanted to draw out of it the truth that is already there.

Who hides in you? What a wonderful question! Though it is not usually the first question we think of, I would encourage people to ask that same question of suffering. "Who hides in you?" In our losses we are invited to stand with faith and to choose to trust that there is *more* here than the pain. Hidden in our suffering is the very love of God.

The question "Why?"—though understandable—is ultimately inadequate. It seems to imply that *God*—separate from us—is sending us suffering for some immediate purpose. But God is much more wonderful than that. Though God does not inflict suffering on us, God does makes "all things work for good" (*Romans 8:28*)—even our pain and loss! Because God has embraced our sufferings, God can give them meaning, and bring from them a much greater good than we can imagine.

In light of the death and resurrection of Jesus, the questions "Why?" and "Why did this happen to me?" need ultimately to give way to the bigger question: *"Now what?"* Given this reality of pain or suffering, *now* how will I live? Can I choose to trust the God who is always working a greater good than what I can see—even from what is to me tragedy and loss? Now what? Now where is love? Now what is called from me? Now how do I go on?

"Mothers Against Drunk Driving" and bereavement groups such as "Compassionate Friends" and "Parents of Murdered Children," are some of the countless examples of the efforts to create a more just and loving world that came from those who faced suffering and loss with the "Now what?" question.

The question has been well phrased: "Will I let myself become *bitter*, or with God's grace, will I let myself become *better?*" Mythologist Joseph Campbell offered the dictum: "You have to give up the life you planned, and find the life that is waiting for you." Our job is to yield to God, to open ourselves so that God can lead us to a new and even deeper life.

The promise is that our crosses are more than obstacles. Our sufferings carry within themselves the promise of transformation, of resurrection. Indeed, it is often the brokenness itself that can help us open our hearts more than we would at other times to truly meet God. Our experiences of limitation can themselves lead us to our Creator.

This is one of the wisdoms of "Alcoholics Anonymous" and other 12-step programs, whose first step is to invite us to accept our powerlessness, and, therefore, our need for a higher power. It is only when we are able to recognize and embrace our weaknesses that we are truly able to let ourselves receive from the one who wanted to help bring us life all along. Our suffering can help us be emptied so that we might be more available to be filled with God!

Humble Birthing

Saint Paul speaks of all creation laboring to give new birth *(Romans 8:22)*. It seems to me that God's role—as author of all life—is not like that of the stork who antiseptically delivers babies by showing up to drop off some wonderfully packaged, clean, and smiling ball of new life. Instead, God is perhaps more like a midwife, getting in the painful mess with us, coaching us, encouraging us, and sustaining us with love. As creator, not only does God call forth a new life but also helps us labor to bring that life to birth.

How humbly, how quietly, God works to birth a new good from our suffering. So humbly does God work that it is usually only later—after we have reflected on it—that we can see what God was doing in the midst of our sorrow to birth new life—in us—and through us.

Glimpses

Sometimes, in our suffering and loss we might get to see a glimpse of God's working among us. Usually, the glimpses we see in our sufferings are simple, not dramatic; often quiet and humble. Perhaps we catch a glimmer of hope in the stranger who smiled . . . maybe for a moment, we sense that our silence touches the silence of God . . . perhaps we recognize God's presence in the breeze that catches our faces on a warm evening . . . maybe we see God's care in the goodness of someone who tries to reach out . . . or even in the compassion in our own hearts.

Such moments don't sound like much, but when we suffer, they can be enough to help open us to trust that there is more to our life than suffering.

Leaping into Darkness

There are other times, however, when it seems that —if there is a God—God must be far away. The world at its core seems to be a cold and silent emptiness. Certainly, Jesus felt alone and abandoned in his pain as he cried from the cross, "My God, my God, why have you forsaken me?" (*Mark 15:34*). There are those times when our losses weigh so heavily on us we can barely breathe. It is hard to imagine that there could be any life on the other end of our grief.

We rightly call it then, a "leap of faith" when we *choose*—like Jesus—to trust. It is a letting go into what seems like darkness.

Once during a house fire, a man crawled out to safety. His daughter stood at the second floor window, trapped and terrified. He called out to her, "Jump, Lisa, jump into my arms!" Because of all the smoke, she couldn't see him, and she cried out, "But, daddy, I can't see you." "It's okay," he said, "because I can see you."

It is our faith that when we cannot see God, God *can* see us and waits with arms opened in love. God never promises that life will be easy, but God promises to always be there—filled with love for us. God is fully engaged with us in every moment of each of our lives, always inviting us to a deeper living, always calling forth—from death—the birth of a new life. When, like Jesus, we make the leap of faith, we find that our daily sufferings, even our very deaths, give way to the birth of a resurrected life.

No matter what life throws at us, no matter what we suffer, we rest in the hope that at the other end of our suffering, God will catch us in the arms of love.

> *"Faith is the bird that feels the light and sings when the dawn is still dark."*
>
> —Rabindranath Tagore

WHY PRAY?

*"When you look for me, you will
find me."–God*

—Jeremiah 29:13

Once a first grade teacher asked her students, "Where does God live?"
The students excitedly raised their hands to give their various answers.
One said, "God lives in nature," and another, "God lives in church." One little girl
suggested, "God lives in our hearts," and the teacher agreed with all their
answers. After a brief pause, a little boy who had several teenage siblings raised
his hand and offered, "God lives in the bathroom of our house." The teacher
paused and then wisely said, "Tell me more about that." The little boy replied,
"Well, almost every morning I hear my dad knocking on the bathroom door
saying, "My God, are you still in there?!"

The answer, quite honestly, is "Yes." The God who created the world and all
that is in it, the God who set the sun in the sky by day and the moon and the
stars by night, does live in the bathroom of that little boy's house. The wonder
is—no matter where we are, or what our life situation might be at the
moment—God is indeed there, filled with love for us!

Every place, every situation, then becomes for us a *sacrament,* a place
where we can meet God: our bathrooms; our friendships; our laughter; even
our suffering; even our sinfulness.

God is always and everywhere present to us. However, we are not always present to God. In prayer, we need to bring ourselves, as we are, with an openness to meet more than ourselves. We develop a way of seeing and hearing that opens us to more than the chattering of our own thoughts and feelings. In prayer, we try to be available to meet *The Other*, the holy one, the source of love.

Words

Interestingly enough, we sometimes say prayers in such a manner as to keep ourselves away from God. Perhaps on some level the idea of actually meeting *The Other* is so overwhelming that we can use religion simply as a way to *feel* prayerful, without having to actually sit authentically in the presence of God.

I chuckled at the story of the young boy who really wanted a bicycle for his birthday. He asked his mom and dad if they could buy him one and they told him, "No, we just don't have the money right now." So the little boy decided he would go right to the top and began to write a letter to God: "Dear God, I promise that if you help me get a bicycle for my birthday, I will be good for one whole year." The little boy realized that that was probably too ambitious, so he crumpled his paper and started over. "Dear God, if you get me a bike for my birthday, I will not fight with my sister for one whole month." Right then his sister came by and stuck her tongue out at him, and he again crumpled his paper, realizing that that probably wasn't going to work either. So the little boy sat and thought awhile and finally came up with an idea. He went into his mother's room where she had a statue of Mary the Blessed Mother on her dresser. He took the statue, wrapped it up in a towel, put it in a shoe box, put the shoe box inside a chest, locked it, placed the chest in the very back of his closet, and locked the closet. Then he took out a piece of paper and began to write a new note to God: "Dear God, if you ever want to see your mother again . . ."

Sometimes we pray that way. We use prayer as if it were a way to manipulate God. For example, we might be told that if we say certain prayers for a specified number of days, then we can be *assured* that God will grant our intention. Unfortunately, such an approach is often all about *us* and our need for control. Though we might be saying prayers, this is not *prayer*. In such an approach, there is little room, if any, for God.

The truth is, we can't make ourselves loveable to God. The wonderful news is that we don't need to—God is already filled with love for us! In our prayer, we come humbly to be with the God who already loves us more than we can imagine. We bring to God all that we are and care about, and let God be God—and ourselves not be. We sit open-handed in prayer that we might know *who* we are and *whose* we are.

What Happens When We Pray?

Certainly, Jesus was a person of prayer, and on more than one occasion, Jesus tells us to pray. What do we expect to happen when we pray? What is the "result" of our prayer?

When I was in college, I drove in an old car with a group of my friends to Colorado from St. Louis. As we headed out on the highway to begin our trip, we decided to take some time for prayer. We thanked God for the time we were to have together, and we asked God to bless us with things like a good trip, and care of the loved ones we were leaving behind. At one point someone said, "And please bless our car; help it run well and get us there safely." From the back seat, Tom prayed in response, "God, I don't believe that you work on car engines. Please help us—no matter how the car runs—to deal with it well." I thought that was interesting, and it prompted a several-hour discussion on how God was—and wasn't—involved in our lives.

During the night, we dropped off to sleep one by one until our driver awakened us in the middle of Kansas with the news, "We're almost out of gas." Anyone who has ever driven highway 70 through Kansas knows you can go a long time without seeing anything that even *looks* like a gas station. After a moment of dazed silence, one of the group said, "Oh God, please let there be a gas station real soon." To which Tom again replied, "God, I don't believe that you are in charge of gas stations. I pray that whether there is or isn't a gas station, you will help us deal with it well." Given the time of the night, our response to Tom was simply to throw our pillows at him. But he had a point: What was God to do? Take out the highway map, snip off an inch or so of the highway, and put it back together, shorter now, so that we would be at a gas station?

Similarly, what does it mean to pray for a baseball team or the outcome of a particular game? What is God to do? Is God going to change the direction of a fly ball, or knock the baseball out of a fielder's hands? What if both teams are praying? What *does* happen when we pray?

In the 29th chapter of Jeremiah 12–14, we hear:

"When you call me, when you go to pray to me, I will listen to you. When you look for me, you will find me. Yes, when you seek me with all your heart, you will find me with you, says the Lord, and I will change your lot."

This is the greatest result of prayer: that when we pray, we will meet God! In prayer, we meet the God who created the world and all that is in it. In prayer, we meet the God who has embraced our every suffering and weeps with us. In prayer, we meet the God who transforms death by a rebirth of life: the God who—on the other end of our suffering—will catch us in the arms of love.

That encounter will change us.

While nothing happens outside the providence of God, the primary arena of God's activity is beyond the length of a highway or the direction of a baseball; the arena is in the human heart.

In prayer, we open ourselves to meet the God who sometimes comes in silence . . . sometimes in fierceness . . . sometimes in a gentle nudge . . . but always in love. The best and truest "result" of authentic prayer is this: when we seek God—we will find God!

What about Miracles?

Certainly, when someone we love is ill or suffering, it is good to bring that person to God in prayer. Such a posture of humbly coming before God in our need can itself open us up to encounter the living God. With or without words, we hold our loved ones and all our cares before God, trusting that God, like a truly loving parent, hears us and is moved.

Many of us have seen times when it seems that such prayer has made a remarkable difference in the lives of those for whom we prayed. Perhaps, for example, we've heard of, or have experienced, the cure of a person through prayer beyond what medicine was able to do for them. Indeed, I know how grateful I am for those times when I have been sustained by the prayers of others.

I do not know how this happens. By focusing the energy of our intentional awareness, perhaps we become more open vessels of God's grace for the world. Certainly, as members of the body of Christ, as we grow, all the body of Christ is blessed.

But we need to take care around the questions of miracles. What does it mean if we pray for someone to be cured of his or her illness, and he or she dies anyway? What does it do to our faith if we don't receive what we hoped for? Or what if we do?

When we look at the life of Jesus, we see that there were indeed miracles. Jesus, however, did not heal all those in need. Some he couldn't because "he was amazed at their lack of faith" *(Mark 6:5–6)*. Some he just didn't. Miracles clearly were not the primary focus of Jesus' ministry. Indeed, Jesus found miracles problematic because people seemed again and again to get caught up in the wrong thing and to miss what he most wanted them to see.

Jesus came to invite people to a whole new way of living and loving. The healings and cures that Jesus accomplished were signs of the in-breaking of the reign of God, and of the ultimate victory of love over hatred, life over death. Jesus wanted his miracles to lead people more deeply into the mystery of God and to living God's way. People's most common response to Jesus' miracles was to look for more miracles, missing the whole point of what Jesus was doing— and what Jesus was inviting them to do.

Miraculous cures do not seem to be the primary work of God now, any more than they were at the time of Jesus. Though God only wants life for us, the reality of our human condition is that all people suffer, all people die. Our faith does not call us to believe that people will be healed of their suffering. Rather, we are called to believe that when someone is suffering, *all the love in the universe* is present to him or her! What the person most deeply needs, he or she already has.

When someone I love is facing a serious illness, I do pray earnestly for him or her. I name to God my hopes and invite God's healing peace to flow through the person's body and spirit. I ask God to guide the doctors, nurses, family members, friends, and all who care for the one who is ill, praying that we might have what we most deeply need to love well in the midst of this. Then, with God's help, I try to fall silent before mystery and let go into the goodness of God beyond what I can see.

A Greater Good

In a striking statement on the way God answers prayers, Jesus said, "If you then, who are wicked, know how to give good gifts to your children, how much more will the Father in heaven give the Holy Spirit to those who ask him?" (*Luke 11:13*). The answer God gives to our prayers is this: God gives us God. Whatever we ask for, God has one answer, and the answer is "God."

When people brought a paralyzed man through the roof to Jesus (*Mark 2:1–12*), it seems likely that they brought him there so that Jesus would cure him. Jesus' response, however, was instead to forgive the man's sins. Though Jesus later also healed him physically (to indicate his power to some Pharisees), had these Pharisees not pushed the point, it is conceivable that Jesus would have stopped with forgiving the man's sins. If we could have interviewed the paralyzed man at this point, I doubt that he would have been upset that instead of physical healing, what he received from Jesus was forgiveness for his sins. Though forgiveness was not what the paralyzed man was asking for, it was what he most needed—the greater good!

So it is in our lives. Which is the greater miracle: that we be healed of a physical infirmity or that we become more loving? In our prayer, it is important to be open to that which is the greater healing.

Henri Nouwen told of a friend of his who was very ill. His friend had a great devotion to Mary and decided to go to Lourdes, France, to ask for healing. Nouwen was afraid that she would be disillusioned if no miracle happened. When she came back she said, "Never did I see so many sick people. When I came face to face with the human suffering, I no longer wanted a miracle. I no longer wanted to be the exception. I experienced a deep desire to be one of them, to belong to these wounded people. Instead of praying for a cure, I prayed that I would have the grace to bear my illness in solidarity with them."

Sometimes when we are looking for a *cure*, we might not see the greater *healing* that God offers. The greatest miracles Jesus worked, and continues to work, are the changing of people's hearts.

Once upon a time a seeker went from land to land to discover authentic religion. He came upon a people known for the goodness of their lives and the sincerity of their worship. The seeker found the master of this group and said,

"I am impressed with what I see, but, first, a question. Does your God do miracles?" The master said thoughtfully, "It depends on what you call a miracle. Some call it a miracle when God does the will of people. We call it a miracle when people do the will of God."

Like Little Children

For those times when I find prayer to be a struggle, I've always appreciated what Thomas Merton, the great spiritual writer said about prayer. He said, "We are always beginners."

Our prayer does not need to be fancy or pretty. It needs to be honest and humble. One young woman I know, who had just buried her husband after his sudden death, said she no longer had any idea how to pray. All she could do was tell God, "I am just here."

That is often all we can do—and that is enough. "I am here, God." Some-times we might say that with a broken heart, maybe angrily, almost defiantly; or perhaps we can barely choke the words out through our tears. It can be a wonderful prayer to simply say, "I am here, God. Here I am."

Sometimes, as in any relationship, it is best that there are no words. Sometimes our prayer can be a silent, trusting presence.

An elderly gentleman passed his granddaughter's room one night and overheard her repeating the alphabet very slowly and reverently. He peeked in and saw her kneeling down next to her bed, her hands folded as if in prayer, slowly and reverently saying, "h, i, j, k, l, m, n, o, p . . ." When she finished, he asked her what she was doing. "I'm saying my prayers," she said. "Oh?" said grandpa. "Well," she explained, "sometimes I can't think of exactly the right words. So I just say all the letters. I know that God will know how to put them together for me in the best way."

She is right. God will indeed put her prayer together in the best way. Such is the childlike faith to which we are all called. In prayer, we meet more than ourselves. We meet the one who would die for us. We meet love.

> *"When you look for me, you will find me."–God*
> —Jeremiah 29:13

PART TWO

Sarte was right: You have to live each moment as if you're prepared to die.

—Anatole Broyard

CHAPTER FIVE

DIGNITY IN LIFE AND IN DEATH

"Not even Solomon in all his splendor
was clothed like one of them."
—Matthew 6:29

A little boy who loved puppies was saving up his money to buy one. Each day he would go to the pet store to play with the puppies. One day he approached the man at the counter, reached into his pocket, pulled out a handful of coins, and laid them on the counter. "Sir, is this enough money to buy a puppy?" "I'm sorry," said the owner. "You only have $1.87, and the puppies are $14.00 apiece."

The little boy sadly put the money back into his pocket and visited a little longer with the puppies. The owner noticed a tear trickling down the little boy's cheek, and something stirred in his heart. He said, "I tell you what, son. You can have a puppy for the money you brought. You go ahead and pick one." The boy's face lit up in anticipation, "Really, sir? Do you mean it?" "Sure, son, go ahead and pick any puppy you want." "Oh, thank you, sir. Thank you, thank you, thank you."

Since he played with the puppies all the time, the little boy knew exactly which one he wanted. As he lifted that puppy out of the cage the owner said, "Now, wait a minute, son. I know I told you that you could have any puppy you wanted, but you don't want that puppy. That puppy is the only one in the group that was born with a bad leg. Why don't you pick a healthy puppy? That puppy will never chase sticks for you or run in the park with you. Why don't you pick a healthy one?"

The little boy said, "It's okay that the puppy has a bad leg." As he said this, he bent over and rolled up his pants leg to reveal his own twisted leg in a metal brace. "You see, I have one, too.

I don't need a puppy that can jump and run in the park because I'll never be able to do that either. All I need, sir, is a puppy that I can love. I promise you, sir, I'll be the best friend to this little puppy."

That young boy reminds me of each of us. We are each "imperfect." There are things about ourselves that we dislike; there are pieces of our past that we wish had never occurred; we've all had to let go of the dreams of how we were sure life "ought" to be. Yet, like that little boy, in the midst of our imperfections, we can love. No weakness, no disability, no suffering destroys that goodness.

Our dignity is this alone— that we *are* loved and *can* love. It does not depend on any of the externals that our society suggests. We live in an age which loudly proclaims that human dignity depends on various external criteria: that we are attractive; successful; healthy; popular; and on and on. This is a great cultural lie.

The same God who said to Jesus at his baptism "You are my beloved," has said that to *us*. We are each "beloved of God." This is our dignity; therefore, our goodness, our worth is intrinsic. It does not end if we feel meaningless, are imprisoned, suffer pain, or are no longer young or attractive. Our dignity is that we are beloved children of God. Period. Even when we cannot remember that, it is true. No one can take that away from us!

Victor Frankl, who survived horrible conditions at both Dachau and Auschwitz concentration camps talked about the fact that, though we are not free from whatever type of conditions others may inflict upon us, we *are* free to choose how we will respond and free to choose our attitude toward life. As he was being stripped of his clothes he said, "You can take away my wife and children and all I have, but you cannot take away my freedom to choose how to respond."

No one can take our dignity from us or our ability to love. Nor does injury or illness rob us of it. The Sacrament of the Anointing of the Sick, which is not reserved only for those in danger of immediate death, calls us forth when we are ill to receive the love and prayers of the community. But it also celebrates the gifts we bring to the community! In this sacrament, we celebrate the dignity that is ours as beloved members of the Body of Christ—even in our illness, even in death.

Not long ago I saw a poem in a parish bulletin that spoke this truth well. Without denying the difficulty and loss of dealing with cancer, the poem acknowledges how much more we are than our illness. The poem, entitled "What Cancer Can't Do," says in part:

Cancer is so limited.
It cannot cripple love.
It cannot kill friendship.
It cannot shut out memories.
It cannot silence courage.
It cannot invade the soul.
It cannot reduce eternal life.
It cannot lessen the power of the resurrection.

How wonderfully put. Our goodness, our worth, is an intrinsic part of who we are by God's grace. It does not end if we are ill, or even if we are dying. Like the boy with the imperfect leg, we can still love. Even when we reach those limitations that mean we can no longer actively do things for others, our dignity is not diminished. Part of our goodness, then, is that we can call love out of others.

Facing Our Own Death

When 80-year-old John Quincy Adams was asked by a friend how he was, he replied, "John is very well, thank you. But the house he lives in is sadly dilapidated. It is tottering on its foundations. The walls are badly shattered and the roof is worn. The building trembles with every wind, and I think John Quincy Adams will have to move out of it before long. But he himself is very well, thank you."

Dignity in Life and in Death

As John Adams understood, even death does nothing to diminish our dignity. Yet, death is not something that most people readily talk about. Many avoid even thinking about the reality of their death. Yet what a great gift for those who do!

Philip of Macedonia gave one of his slaves a strange order. Every day this slave was to march into the king's chamber unannounced, and no matter what the king was doing, proclaim in a loud voice, "You are going to die!"

The king knew that he needed such a reminder to help him keep his perspective on life. Such a reminder might help transform us as well. An awareness of the shortness of our lives provides urgency to our living: What really matters? Am I living *now* those values that live forever?

Sometimes we get so caught up in things which, while seeming to be very important at the time, mean very little in light of the shortness of life. I've been at the bedside of many people as they faced the reality of their upcoming death. As they looked back over their lives, never once did I hear things such as, "If I could live my life over again, I'd have spent more time at the office," or "My one regret is that I don't have a bigger stock portfolio." Facing the reality of our own death invites us to wake up to how we live *now*.

One morning years ago, Alfred Nobel, the man who invented dynamite, sat down to have a cup of coffee, opened his newspaper, and to his surprise read his own obituary! A reporter had mistakenly reported Alfred's death in place of his brother's. As you could imagine, Alfred was shocked. But it gave him the fascinating opportunity to read what was written about him and how he would be remembered. His obituary described him accurately as the "dynamite king" who had spent his life making instruments of death and destruction.

This was not the legacy that Alfred Nobel wanted to leave the world. That morning, Alfred Nobel resolved to change his life. He changed the direction of his life so dramatically that after his death, annual prizes would be awarded in physics, chemistry, medicine, literature, and peace in his name. He went from being the "dynamite king" to the one for whom the "Nobel Peace Prize" was named.

Such is the gift of facing the reality of our own death. Perhaps we might imagine what would be written about us if we died. Or, better yet, perhaps we would do well to compose our own obituary. If we had the opportunity to write an article about ourselves to be published after we died, what would we want to say about ourselves? What would we want to be noted for?

To think for a moment about how I want to be remembered after death confronts me with the question, "How am I living *now*?" If I want my legacy to be that I was a person who cared for others, a person of prayer, or someone who loved my family, I would do well to examine whether or not I am living those values *now*. Facing the reality of our deaths provides a chance to choose again what really matters.

End-of-Life Medical Care

It is vitally important to plan for the physical reality of death. Adults need to make out a will and to take care of financial and other obligations. But it is crucial that we also complete advance medical directives and a living will, and discuss these wishes with our family. What medical treatment would I want if I had no hope of regaining consciousness or if I was near death? What would the benefits of such treatment be? The burdens? Whom do I most trust to make my health care decisions when I no longer have the capacity to make them? It is important to put these wishes in writing.

Similarly, we would also do well to sign our organ donation cards, and let family and friends know our wishes with regard to the use of our organs to help another person's life. In taking care of such end-of-life directives, we acknowledge our true dignity before God, while sparing our families much confusion at a difficult time.

There are two extremes to be avoided in making decisions about end-of-life medical care. The first extreme is to reject all types of potentially life saving treatment just because we cannot bear the thought of disability. The Jesuit priest Father John Kavanaugh was discussing the issue of doctor-assisted suicide during a class he taught on medical ethics. One of his students said, "I wouldn't want to live if I lost my dignity." Kavanaugh asked him, "And when would that be?" The young man replied, "If I were incontinent." Kavanaugh asked, "Is that our dignity? That we can control a sphincter muscle?" Kavanaugh then went on to teach of the dignity of the human person, a dignity that has nothing to do with what we can or can't do physically.

The second extreme is the scrupulous approach that "everything must be done," insisting on treatments that will prolong dying and may increase suffering. Fortunately, the medical profession is making strides in helping alleviate pain at the end of life. No one with a terminal illness should have to be in avoidable physical pain as they are dying. And love does not call us to endlessly prolong life.

Dying Well

Death is not merely something that happens *to* us, but is an act in which *we* are engaged as well. For example, when Cardinal Joseph Bernardin found that he had terminal cancer, he did not take this as something to passively receive but as a new call in his ministry. Aware of the likelihood of his impending death, he chose to offer his final chapter of life for the service of others. He was an active participant in his own dying, choosing to offer what he learned and experienced for the good of others. Cardinal Bernardin died well.

In my priesthood I have been blessed to see many people die well. When facing their upcoming death, they were *intentional* about how they lived their remaining time. As they were able, they did their best to do the following things:

- Instead of trying to "be strong" for friends and family, they brought relationships to completion by saying those necessary things like: "I forgive you," "I'm sorry," "Thank you," and "I love you."
- In spoken and/or written word they passed on their wisdom and stories as much as they could.
- They let others care for them.
- Finally they let go into the arms of the One who first loved them.

This is "dying with dignity." It is something we learn to do *now*. The more we remember now who we are and where our dignity lies, the less we cling to that which is not true. In truth, the time to learn to let go is *now*. The more we learn *now* to yield our egos and embrace all the "daily little deaths" that love calls of us, the more prepared we are for the death at the end of life. As we grow in relationship to God, death usually becomes less frightening and more of a "going home" to a love we have already tasted here.

Facing the Death of One We Love

Sometimes a loved one dies suddenly and without warning. The awareness of such a possibility is a stark invitation to live well the time we have now and to say now those things that really matter. There are, however, some situations in which we have advance knowledge that someone we love is facing death. This awareness, while heartrending and filled with many challenges, also provides great opportunity.

There is much we can learn from someone who is dying; there is much we have to offer. Those with the courage and love to walk this journey with a loved one who is dying find that much will be called out of them—and much given to them. The experience of death can be transforming, not only to the one who is dying but also to those who journey with him or her. It is a great and painful grace.

There is much wisdom to the old saying: "If you can't add days to a person's life, add life to the person's days." When someone we love is facing death, we have the opportunity to help add life to his or her days. To do this, we need to be intentional about how we will live the time remaining.

Earlier we named some of the important tasks of dying well. The tasks are very similar for loving well someone who is dying. Again, as much as we are able, we do the following things:

- Instead of trying to "be strong" for the one who is dying, we bring our relationship to completion by saying those necessary things like: "I forgive you," "I'm sorry," "Thank you," and "I love you."
- We listen to his or her wisdom and stories.
- We care for the person who is dying, and also *receive* his or her care.
- Finally, we let the dying person go into the arms of the One who first loved him or her.

Unfortunately, we too often let fear rob us of the potential of these days. Sometimes we are afraid of talking and thinking about death for fear that we might take away a person's hope. Keeping hope is good. However, when death is likely, we need to be willing to let our hope be opened to the reality of death, that we might be available for the *healing* that is greater than a *cure*.

The greatest gift we have to offer someone who faces death is our loving presence. They do not need religious clichés. They do not need someone trying to "cheer them up." They need us, as we are, with a willingness to be with them as they are.

That is why one of the most important things we can do is to listen. We must not presume that we know what is best for the one who is dying, but rather listen to him or her. If we truly listen, he or she will provide us clues about their personal needs, including their desire to talk about the various issues that confront him or her. Often, a person is aware that their illness will likely end in death, and are willing, even anxious to talk about it. *Our* fear, however, sometimes prevents them from doing so.

We give a priceless gift to someone who is dying if we provide him or her with an opportunity to talk about their hopes, fears, regrets, and joys at the end of their life. It is not morbid, but actually life-giving, to talk about dying, funeral preferences, and other end-of-life issues.

Part of the essential listening, then, is paying attention to what is going on inside ourselves when caring for someone who is facing death. Perhaps it is our own fears, awkwardness, or other issues that might keep us from doing what most needs to be done in that moment. We need to listen to what is happening inside of ourselves, so that we are aware enough to freely choose to respond in the most loving way. It is also important, whenever possible, to make sure we get good nutrition, exercise, and sleep. In all of this, we become better caregivers through whom God's grace flows.

Hospice is an invaluable gift in this entire process. I continue to be inspired by the blessings hospice provides for someone who is facing terminal illness, and for his or her family. Hospice offers skilled professionals dedicated to helping people die with dignity, and to helping the whole family be a loving part of that process. Using their experience and wisdom, hospice personnel help make sure that the one who is dying is comfortable and respected; they provide information about all aspects of the dying process; and they assist everyone involved in choosing how to live well the time they have. I hope that all those I love will know to utilize the gift of hospice when facing their own death or the death of someone they love.

Tangible Presence

There is no need to try to protect the one who is dying from our tears. It is okay if we cry, for our tears can help show we care. Indeed, Jesus wept at the death of his friend Lazarus! (*John 11:35*) The tears of family members, friends, and helping professionals might also help provide permission for the one who is dying to embrace his or her own emotions more directly.

Some people find themselves embarrassed by their tears. Several months after my friend Vivian's death, I was talking about her with one of my friends and found myself crying. I apologized, but my friend wisely said, "Oh, that's okay. You wouldn't cry if you didn't love her." I'm glad he said that. Over the years, I have come to understand that tears of letting go are "holy water" because they come from love.

Again, the most healing gift we can give is our honest, loving presence. Sometimes we are present in silence; sometimes with tears; and sometimes through our touch.

Touch can be wonderfully healing to someone who is facing death. Someone who is already grappling with the loneliness of death can feel even more isolated by those who stand at arm's length. Holding the hand or touching the arm of someone willing to be touched can be tremendously comforting when one is feeling the separation of death. As her father was dying, my friend Peggy climbed into the bed with him to hold him. She will always be grateful that she took that opportunity.

As the time of death draws near, it seems that the veil between this world and the next is very thin, and that sometimes the person who is dying moves back and forth between the two. Our loving presence continues to be a gift at this time. In the final stages of a person's dying, it is good to presume that he or she can still hear us. We do well to continue to love the dying person with our touch, our silence, our tears, and our words of love, prayers, and encouragement. We trust that, on some level, the person who is dying can still hear us and is aware of our love.

Sometimes, it is important to tell a loved one who is dying that it is "okay to let go." Those words of permission, along with our love, forgiveness, and prayer can help the dying person move from the love in this life to the love that awaits him or her in the next.

Solidarity

As beloved children of God, we have a noble dignity—in our living, and in our dying. Essential to understanding this dignity is the truth that we belong to *a people!* Our lives are not all about us: we are part of something much bigger than ourselves. In our suffering, we can sometimes feel alone, for there is such a lonely nature to pain. But we do not suffer—or die—alone. In ways beyond our understanding, when we suffer, we share a deep, deep solidarity with God and with one another. Because Baptism immerses us into the death of Jesus, our sufferings and death are no longer simply "our own private story," but are part of the "big story," the suffering of the Body of Christ.

This is often difficult to remember in the midst of the suffering. That is why it is so important to build into our lives the support of the church community. It is hard to remember who we are in a world that tells us our very worth depends on how individually successful we are, how we look, or how popular we are. It is in the wisdom and love of the church community that we can remember who we are and where our dignity lies. When we suffer and when we die, we can touch, in the love of the Church community, the presence of the God who suffers with us and will never abandon us.

Often it is those whom the world disregards who teach us of our true dignity. At the Special Olympics, a group of young men with Down's syndrome was running around the track in their big race when one of the racers near the back tripped and fell, crying out in pain as he scraped his knee. The runner who was leading the race heard the other youth's cries and stopped and turned around. When he saw the young man down on the track, he started to walk back toward his fellow racer. The other runners also stopped. When the first youth reached his fallen companion, he helped him to his feet and said, "It's okay." The first youth put his arm around the second youth's shoulder and started walking with him toward the finish line. Soon the other runners joined them, locked arms, and walked the final part of the race together. With the crowd on its feet enthusiastically cheering them on, the group of runners together walked across the finish line arm in arm. They were all winners.

So it is with all of us. Together we walk arm in arm in our weaknesses toward the finish line, beloved children of God, in our deepest dignity.

> *"Not even Solomon in all his splendor*
> *was clothed like one of them."*
>
> —Matthew 6:29

CHAPTER SIX

THE BIRTH THAT IS
DEATH–LIFE AFTER LIFE

"I have called you by name:
you are mine."—God
—Isaiah 43:1

Once there were twins in their mother's womb. They were very happy there, for it was warm and cozy, and safe. They played games all day, and often stayed up late into the night telling stories. Sometimes they were quiet, simply listening to each other's heartbeats and enjoying the comfort of each other's presence.

One day, there was tremendous upheaval and great turmoil. When things settled down a bit, and the one twin opened his eyes again, he saw to his horror that his brother was gone. He was both frightened and heartbroken. Not only was this his twin that was gone but also his best friend. Now he was alone. Now, he no longer had his brother with whom to play games. He had no one with whom to stay up late into the night and tell stories. How empty the womb seemed now; how dark and lonely.

What he did not realize was that his brother had been born! He could not see the loving arms that were there to welcome his brother at his birth. He did not see the tears of joy in his mother and father's eyes that their child had been born to them. He did not really understand what it meant "to be born." All he knew was that his brother was gone, and the world seemed terribly empty and sad.

So it is for us with the death of a loved one. When someone we love dies, our world seems empty and cold. We think our loved one should be there, and we look—but they are gone. We long to see them, to talk and laugh with them. We yearn to hold them again and to know that they are okay. We ache with our loss. It is as if part of us has died.

But, like that twin still in his mother's womb, what we do not see is that our loved one has been born! We don't see the arms of God who welcomes our loved one home—or the tears of joy that the one we love has been born.

In the resurrection of Jesus, we rest our hope in that which we cannot see. In the darkness of our loss, we cling to the promise of a life beyond this life. Our faith does not remove the pain of our loss, but helps us to trust that *death, too, is a birth.*

The Indian Jesuit Tagore once described the beauty of the evening sky as "a window and a lighted lamp, and a waiting behind it." Our faith tells us that that "waiting" is God, surrounded by the saints, ready and waiting with outstretched arms to welcome us home. As the Catholic funeral liturgy says, "Life is changed, not ended, and when the body of our earthly dwelling lies in death, we gain an everlasting dwelling place in heaven."

Our belief in the resurrection of the body sustains our hope for our unity with our loved ones beyond this life. Heaven, however, is not a physical place "up there," but rather a state of complete union with all that is love. Most attempts to imagine the beauty of such communion with God will fall short. Saint Paul tells us that life beyond this life will be even more wonderful than we can ever imagine, "What eye has not seen, and ear has not heard, and what has not entered the human heart, what God has prepared for those who love him" *(1 Corinthians 2:9).* We do, however, get glimpses. There are those moments *now* that carry within themselves the promise of that which is eternal. The unmerited grace of friendship, the beauty of simple goodness, the astonishing gift of forgiveness, and other such blessings offer glimpses in this life of the beauty of the life to come.

Yes, there is a life beyond this life. At death, we are birthed into the arms of love.

Death Does Not End a Relationship

The great Easter promise of life beyond death helps us know that, even now, we are connected with our loved ones who have died. Just because someone we love dies does not mean that our relationship with them has ended. Though we no longer see them, we are still deeply united. Nothing can keep love from being communicated, not even death.

We pray for our loved ones who have died, not to convince God to love them, for God already does that more than we can imagine. Rather, our love and prayers are an aid toward their completion, to empower them to open up more to receive the embrace of God's great healing love. Not only do we pray for them; they also pray for us.

Coach Lou Little at Columbia University tells about the time when a freshman, who was not an exceptional football player, tried out for the football team. Though his skills were not tremendous, the young man had a lot of heart and enthusiasm, and the coach decided to keep him on the team. He figured that the kid wouldn't play very much, but that his enthusiasm and spirit would likely be a good influence on the other players. That was how it turned out. As time went on, the coach developed an affection for the kid. He used to watch him walking arm-in-arm with his father across the campus, and would see them at Church together on Sundays.

One day a call came that the young man's father had died, and the coach was to break the news to the son. They sat down together, and the coach told him the news. Afterwards, they talked for a long time. As the young man prepared to leave for the funeral, the coach again expressed his sympathy and offered to do anything he could to help.

The young man left to bury his father. Several days later, he returned, and the young man met again with the coach. He said, "Coach, remember when you told me to let you know if there was anything you could do for me? There is something I want. I'd like to start in Saturday's game."

The coach hesitated. He would, of course, keep his word, but he also was very aware that this was the biggest game of the year. Coach decided to keep him in the game for several plays and then take him out. On the first play from scrimmage, though, the young man made an outstanding play. It did not stop there. Much to the coach's surprise, he went on to play so well that the coach decided to keep him in the whole game. The young man ended up receiving a game ball for being one of the best players in the game.

As soon as the game was over, coach asked him, "Son, you've never played that well before. Tell me, what got into you today?" The young man said, "Coach, you know that I really loved my dad. What most people didn't realize was that he was blind. When you would see us walking around campus arm-in-arm, I was helping guide him. It was on the way back from his funeral that I realized that this game would be the first time Dad would ever see me play."

Death does not end a relationship. Our loved ones who have gone before us grow more alive in God, and are in a very real way "cheering us on," pulling for us, praying for us. It is good to pray for our loved ones who have died and to receive from them their love and prayers.

Yes, like the twin whose brother was born, when someone we love dies, our world seems empty. In faith, we hold on to the great truth that beyond this life there is a "waiting," and death itself is a birth.

"I have called you by name: you are mine."–God
—Isaiah 43:1

TO GRIEVE

"Blessed are they who mourn . . ."—Jesus
—Matthew 5:4

A friend of mine named Jim accurately described the timeline for grief. He said, "We buried our eleven-year-old daughter Deborah Ann over thirty years ago. We still miss her. When people ask me, 'When do you get over it?' my answer is, 'I don't know.' "

When someone we love dies, or when we suffer any major loss, we do not "get over it." Our lives are changed forever. We figure out how to continue. We learn new ways to be okay, but we will never be the same.

There are many different changes and losses that can elicit grief. Divorce, a chronic illness, the death of a pet, the inability to conceive a child, a job loss, an unwanted move, and countless other losses lead to grief. Our grief responses have many similarities no matter what the source of the losses.

However, since death is such a universal suffering, the focus here will be to look at grief from the perspective of one who has experienced the death of a loved one.

No One Cries the Wrong Way

When someone we love dies, our lives are changed forever. There is a pain and a loneliness in grief at the death of a loved one that is perhaps unimaginable— except to those who have themselves lost deeply. It has been accurately said that no one ever really can understand.

From the loneliness of the drive in the funeral procession when other cars pass by as if nothing has happened to going through the possessions of the loved one who has died; from the emptiness of holidays, birthdays, anniversaries, and all those things our loved ones used to be a part of to the pain of watching other family members grieve; from waking up in the middle of the night and crying because we ache to hold our loved one again to the growing awareness that he or she is never walking into our arms again— at the death of a loved one we are confronted with the reality that life is changed forever.

People who suggest, "You should be over it by now" are likely either to be people who have never experienced a tragedy, or who have denied their own pain through repression.

Knowing that there is life beyond this life can give us peace in the midst of the loss, but it does *not* take away our emptiness and pain. For many, it is as if someone reached inside of us and pulled out a big piece of our heart.

There is an exceptionally misguided notion that in response to the death of a loved one, we are to "be strong," to keep ourselves together, and to hold our emotions in check. This is not true. It is vitally important that we allow ourselves to honestly experience our grief reactions. Grief ignored or denied comes at a great price.

Sometimes we compare our suffering with another's and tell ourselves we ought not to grieve, saying, "I know that there are people a lot worse off than me." Knowing that others suffer is a good perspective to have. One of the steps toward wholeness can be to acknowledge the pain of others and reach out to them in love. But the fact that others are suffering does not take away our loss, which is itself real and important to be grieved.

How we grieve is affected by many things, including what our relationship was like with the person who died, the level of support we have from others, the messages about grief and coping we learned growing up, and how our loved one died. Grief after a long slow illness is similar to, but also different grief after a sudden or unexpected death.

How we grieve will vary according to how different each of us are. There is no correct way to grieve and no time limit. When his younger sister died at sixteen years of age, a young man named Jimmy described it well when he said, "No one cries the wrong way." And no one can accurately tell us, "I know just how you feel."

Common Grief Reactions

Though no one grieves in exactly the same way, there are, however, many things that are commonly experienced. Often there is consolation simply in knowing that we are not the first—nor the last—to experience some of what we feel.

It is almost universal that people who are grieving will experience a whole mixture of thoughts and emotions. I encourage those who are grieving not to try to *predict* how they should feel at any given moment, but rather to simply experience what they feel when they feel it. Sometimes we can be surprised by our own reactions—or lack of them.

The following are direct quotes from people who have had a loved one die. They represent just a few of the many things that I have heard repeated in one form or another by many people grappling with their loss:

- At first I just couldn't believe it. I kept thinking that maybe I would wake up, and it would all be a dream.
- Each morning, I would wake up with the vague feeling that something was wrong. And then I would open my eyes and remember he's gone, and start crying again.
- It is so hard to eat. There's this knot in my stomach that won't go away.
- Sometimes for a while, I forget that she died. Then something reminds me, and it rips my heart apart all over again.
- Sometimes I still expect him to walk in through that door.

- I feel so helpless. I watch everyone around me in such pain, and there is nothing I can do. I can barely get myself dressed.

- Every time I have to tell someone else that she died, my heart breaks again.

- No one in my family understands what it is like for me.

- Though we were at her bedside most of the time, I think she waited until no one was around to die.

- I'm afraid that once I start crying, I'll never be able to stop.

- Though I never really thought much about it, I always thought that there was life after death. Since my child died, now I sometimes get scared and wonder, "What if it isn't true? What if there is no God?"

- I hardly cried at the funeral. Several days later, I was standing in front of the frozen food counter at the store when I suddenly burst into tears.

- I found myself wanting to kill anyone who was happy.

- They kept telling me to have faith. Now I feel guilty. Maybe if I had had enough faith, she would have been healed.

- When I saw others crying at the funeral home, it made me mad. Didn't they know that this was hardest on me?

- At nighttime I keep dreaming about him. Sometimes I get confused about whether or not I'm dreaming.

- I told him he should watch what he eats; but he didn't, and now he's dead. I should have watched him more closely.

- It is hard for me to admit, but I'm angry *at him* for dying. He has it fine now, while the rest of us have to try to muddle through.

- People tell me they know exactly how I feel. No, they don't. They have no idea.

- I didn't think I could take it and thought about killing myself.

- We had one of those little arguments that morning. If only I had told him that I loved him before he left that morning.

- I hope this isn't wrong, but I'm glad he died.

Chapter Seven

- I feel like I am going crazy.
- I don't cry on the outside; my tears are in my heart.
- I feel like I'm now part of a club I never wanted to join.
- At first we prayed for a miracle. In the end, we didn't want her to suffer any more, and just prayed that she could die and be at peace.
- Our family fights more now then we used to. It's like we're all in our own worlds.
- At my dad's funeral it looked like everyone was sad. Not me. I was mad at him for never being the father I needed.
- Since dad died I've noticed unusual moments in nature; times when animals came surprisingly close to me. I wondered if it wasn't connected to my dad's death.
- I keep picturing him suffering, and can't get that image out of my head.
- People tell me how strong I am but I don't want to be strong.
- It feels flat, like something inside me has died.
- I just wish I could know for sure that he is okay now.
- I'm so afraid that someone else I love will die.
- When I watch people go on with their lives as usual, I get mad. Don't they know that the world is changed forever?
- It is hard for me to reach out to others, when I'm used to having her understand from across the table.
- I dread the holidays.
- I thought I'd never be happy again.
- It was wonderful that so many people came by or helped out after his death. I didn't realize how much we were loved.
- I thought that if I smiled or laughed, people might think bad of me.
- After my son's death, at first I didn't know how to answer when someone asked me how many children I have. Now I tell them, "I have

four children: three living on earth, one living in heaven."

- Even though she died, for some reason, I still find it helpful to talk to her.

- The first Christmas was the worst. It's still hard now, three years later, but we've developed a new way of celebrating the holidays.

- Sometimes I'm mad if people ask how I'm doing. Sometimes, I'm mad if they don't.

- People act like I should be "over it," but I don't think six years is a long time to be heartbroken.

- Sometimes I'm surprised at the smallest thing that can make me start to cry. Sometimes, I'm surprised that I'm not crying.

- At first, I could only picture him like he was as he was dying. Now, I mostly picture him healthy and happy.

- I wonder if I'm betraying her if I laugh. Am I wrong to be happy again?

- The next time I hear that someone's parent died, I'll react differently. Now I understand.

- Some days I don't feel as sad as I used to; and I miss it.

- I don't think about her all the time. Her life and death are now just a part of who I am.

Perhaps you have heard, or expressed, comments like the above. Though no one grieves in exactly the same way, there are dimensions of the grief experiences that are fairly universal. The most common dimensions of the grief experience include periods of:

- shock, denial, numbness, disbelief
- disorganization, confusion
- danger, frustration, struggle
- anxiety, panic, fear
- depression, hopelessness
- guilt, remorse, yearning
- loss, emptiness, sadness

Often we have reactions to our reactions. For example, perhaps we feel guilty that we are feeling some relief that the person died. Maybe we feel scared by how much anger we are feeling. Maybe we feel sad about how sad we are. It is common to have emotional reactions to our emotional reactions.

Certainly, we can have seemingly contradictory feelings simultaneously. When my own dad died, I experienced seemingly opposite emotions at the same time. Woven into the midst of the deep pain was a beauty and goodness that were almost tangible to me. I tasted the love of family and friends, and the gift of faith. These did not take away the heartache and tears. Nor did the pain cancel out the beauty. Both existed side by side. In grief, we are called to live it all.

At times, I've celebrated weddings for families who have recently buried a loved one. I encourage these families to acknowledge their loss, and not pretend that the joy of the wedding should take away the pain. Similarly, I remind them that it is right to feel joy and to celebrate all that is happy about this day. We do ourselves harm if we try to force either feeling out of the picture.

Complicating Grief

There are many situations that complicate our grieving process and give us even more to work through. Grief is complicated when the bereaved was part of the cause of the death, when the death was considered particularly untimely, when the relationship was troubled, or when more than one person died. There is a cumulative nature to grief, and various losses often seem to "add up" inside us. There are often secondary losses that also need to be dealt with, such as the loss of income or the loss of a home. Perhaps the media is involved, or there are legal problems or police investigations. Sometimes, we don't get to see the body of the loved one who died, and so closure is more difficult.

In some situations there seems to be less permission to grieve. When someone loses an unborn child through miscarriage, abortion, or stillbirth, some seem to imply that the person shouldn't grieve, suggesting things like, "At least you know you can have another child." Yet, the bereaved person is often thinking, "But I wanted *this* baby." It is indeed important to grieve for children who died before or during childbirth. It is often good to give the child a name, entrust that child to God in prayer, and do other rituals of grief and remembering, just as we would for someone who lived longer.

Grief can be especially complicated for the family members and friends of someone who died because of suicide. Grief in this situation is often accompanied by anger at the person who took his or her own life, and guilt that we did not do something to prevent the person's death. Though their grief is just as real, those who survive the loss of a family member or friend to suicide often feel less support than those whose loved one died from some other cause.

There are many other factors that complicate our grief work. Sometimes, it is all we can do to just keep going. Terry Anderson, as chief Middle East correspondent for the *Associated Press,* was working in Beirut in March of 1985 when he was kidnapped off a street and held hostage in Lebanon for almost seven years. He spent much of that time blindfolded and chained. After his release, he was asked how he survived his ordeal. Perhaps those who are grieving can understand his answer, "You just do what you have to. You wake up every day, and you summon up the energy from somewhere, even when you think you haven't got it, and you get through the day. And you do it day after day after day."

Our Role in the Grief Process

Grief is not something that simply happens to us. Grieving is an active, lifelong process in which *we* have an essential role.

To talk about "stages of grief" is misleading, because it seems to suggest that there is an ordered progression that needs to be followed, and a beginning and an end to grief. It is more accurately said that, in addition to the various emotions and other dimensions of the grief experience, there are some *grieving tasks* that we need to accomplish. Though we do not necessarily *consciously* work on these tasks, healthy grief work leads us through them over time.

These tasks could be most simply summarized as threefold:

1. We experience our pain and, over time, accept the reality of our loss. As we move between periods of disbelief, sorrow, and numerous other emotions, the truth of our loss and its consequences becomes clearer and we accept it as reality.
2. We "relearn" how to live in a world that has been changed forever by our losses. What is "normal" is now different, and we figure out how to continue. We learn new ways to function and be okay.

3. We reconcile the death of our loved one into our living. While not denying our loss, we find a renewed meaning and purpose for our lives. Our experience of grief now becomes a part of what we bring to the world.

There are many aspects to each of these dimensions of grieving. They are not tasks that we intentionally set about to achieve, but rather small steps that we painfully accomplish in our daily living by hard work, the care of others, and the grace of God. There are no shortcuts, and one should not try to "get this over with." There are, however, some actions we can take to help ourselves along the way. Below are just a few of the things that many people have found helpful:

- If possible, before, and at the hour of death, say those things that you want to say to your loved one.

- If given the opportunity, after death, spend time with the body of your loved one who died. If there are things you wish you had said earlier, say them now.

- Gather family members together for some family time to remember and tell stories of the person's life. (Perhaps a volunteer could answer the phone and door to help give you the quiet time you need.) As much as possible, keep a balance of nutrition, sleep, and exercise throughout the grieving process

- Help plan and participate in the funeral services. Choose, if possible, to actually be at the graveside for the burial.

- Where available, allow yourself to receive the support of family, friends, your church community, and people trained in understanding grief.

- Keep a journal of your memories (including the dying, the funeral, the days after, and so on).

- Decide on rituals that you will use as an individual, or as a family, to help remind you of your loved one. (For example, a special candle at meal prayers, a memory table, and so on.)

- Write a letter to the loved one who died, to God, or to yourself.

- Do one or more of those things that the person who died loved to do.

- Plant a tree or a flowering plant in your loved one's name, or create a memorial.

- Do something loving for others in honor of your loved one.

These are but a few of the things that have often proven helpful. Some people find great comfort being in nature, while others take extra time to read. As much as possible, it is important to choose whatever we know usually helps us. Since addictive or destructive behaviors will only make things worse, we need to choose those things we've experienced in our lives that help us keep ourselves together. Perhaps, as with prayer, the best we can do is be available for the healing that comes through grace over time.

In response to the death of a loved one, and all that it stirs up inside us, we need to remember that it is okay to laugh and be happy. It is also okay to weep. It is okay to miss a loved one the rest of our lives.

Letting Ourselves Receive

It is important not to grieve all by ourselves. We can tend to let our sufferings isolate us. Perhaps we don't want to be a burden, or maybe we think no one understands. However, Jesus never meant us to suffer alone. One of the greatest challenges we face when we experience loss or pain is to let it connect us with one another. Rather than trying to do it all by ourselves, we are called to let ourselves receive.

If people call and offer to help, I encourage those who are grieving to let them do so. Friends and neighbors who are aware of the loss often feel helpless, and are usually *grateful* for the chance to help in any way. We give our friends and relatives a great gift by being willing to receive from them.

Certainly, the support of friends is priceless. As much as possible, it is important to develop healthy friendships before times of crisis. Often, however, the grieving need to help teach their friends how to be there for them. No one can read anyone else's mind. Though it's hard to do, it is important for those who are grieving to ask for what they need. For example, though many find great blessing in talking about their loved one who died, some friends will be afraid to bring up the deceased's name for fear of causing more pain. Perhaps these friends need to be taught that the tears of the bereaved are not necessarily to be avoided, but rather are part of the healing process.

Also, many have found great blessing in bereavement groups. There is a solidarity in pain, and often hearing the stories of others who grieve provides an important and healing perspective.

Often a trusted counselor is crucial. For example, the death of a child is often extremely difficult for married couples. For a variety of reasons, the death of a child can often pull a couple apart. The percentage of couples that end up divorcing after the death of a child is high. It is often important for a couple to find a trustworthy counselor to walk with them through their grieving process and to help manage its impact on their marriage.

Certainly, if we are able to root our loss in our faith community, we are blessed. Many find it painful to try to pray again after the death of a loved one. What a gift it can be to have the support of other believers who can believe for us when it is hard for us to do so; who can pray for us when it is hard for us to pray. It is one of the jobs of the faith community to sustain us with their prayers, and surround us in their love.

At Sunday Mass on the first Father's Day after my dad died, I found myself fighting back tears when we prayed an intercession for all of our fathers who had died. I slipped into the sacristy to compose myself while the offering was being collected, and then came back out to continue Mass as usual. Afterwards, a woman who had been a great support to me throughout the time of my dad's death challenged me. "Is that what you want to communicate to us? Are you suggesting that when we are sad we should take our grief away from the community to deal with it?" She was right. I did not want to communicate that. God does not intend us to grieve by ourselves. Though no one can take away our loss, God gives us one another that we might not have to walk the journey alone. One of our challenges in grief is to find, and especially to receive, healthy loving support.

Children Grieve, Too

Children also grieve. I can still picture a young boy whose older brother had died, saying with tears in his eyes, "I wish people would talk about *me* sometimes." It is good to think about how children grieve, and about how to best respond to them in their loss.

There is an unfortunate tendency to attempt to hide the realities of suffering and death from children. Both the events of birth and death have been removed from people's homes and now usually happen in hospitals. Despite tremendous advances in hospice and in-home care, few dying patients spend their final days in the comfort of their own home surrounded by family. Children are often denied the opportunity to say their final farewells to a loved one, and are then often excluded from the funeral home, cemetery, and funeral rites.

By attempting to shield children from the realities of suffering and death, we do not protect them. In reality, we hinder their emotional and spiritual growth.

Certainly, it is important that we be honest with our own grief when around children. The idea of "being strong for the children," and not letting them know that we are sad is a terrible one. It is fine to cry in front of the children, for in this we teach them how to grieve. In our honesty, we give them permission to have their own emotions and to do the grief work they need to do.

Some children find benefit in images from nature such as that of a caterpillar transformed into a butterfly or a snake shedding its skin. Certainly, it is extremely important that we take some time to decide what we want to say—and what we don't want to say—when talking with children about death.

Children are often very literal. Many of the typical things that people say without thinking are confusing or harmful to children. Telling children that the one who died "fell asleep" often creates anxiety about sleeping. We tell children, and rightly so, that our loved ones are still with us in spirit. Yet, if we say "Daddy is always watching over you," some children will worry that daddy physically sees everything they do. Telling children that the deceased is "in the ground" is not accurate, since we only bury the body. Some children will then worry about whether or not the person can breathe. Nor should it ever be said that "God needed another angel," or "God only takes the good ones," because such phrases mislead children about God.

It is vital that children have someone trustworthy to talk with about death. They, too, have a mixture of emotions and reactions. We need to let them ask their questions, and in response, give simple, honest answers, remembering that it is okay to say, "I don't know."

Children often ask questions that might surprise us in their honesty. At funeral homes, children sometimes wonder where the legs of the deceased are, since often only the top part of the casket is open. When my cousin's grandma died, he went to the funeral home with his family. When he saw his grandma in the casket with a rosary around her hands as is sometimes done at

Catholic wakes, he asked, "If she's dead, why do they have to chain up her hands like that?" Simple honest answers help give children permission to ask the other bigger things that are in their hearts.

When her grandmother died, one little girl wondered why her mother was crying since Grandma was now in heaven. When she asked, her mother answered, "I know Grandma is happy in heaven. I just miss her here."

It is good to keep in mind that it is not unusual for children to blame themselves for the death of someone they knew. If a child was ever mad at Mommy and thought, "I wish she were dead" that child could believe it was his or her fault that their mother died.

We also need to remember that when children hear discussion about death, they often become frightened that Mom, Dad, or someone else they love might die. While we cannot promise them that this would not happen, we can assure them that usually people are older when they die, and that the children do not need to be afraid.

Children process things differently according to their age and temperament. Younger children have a short attention span and can go from weeping to playing in a very short time. This is fine and we need not shame them for this. Though children are usually resilient, they will likely revisit their grief anew at different times in their development, but in a different way, according to their age.

Helps for Children

Typically, I highly encourage people to bring children to the hospital, the funeral home, the funeral service, and the cemetery. All of these can help bring closure and needed perspective for the children. Children have vivid imaginations, and can often create images of all of this that are much more frightening than the reality.

It is often good to let children pick out some things of the deceased for their very own as "linking objects." A memory box of such items can help by providing a tangible connection to the deceased and a focal point for their memories.

Drawing a picture for, or writing a note to the person who died can be very helpful for children.

Using clay, paint, or other materials can help children express that for which they have no words. If the children draw or make something, I've learned that I should not presume that I understand what they have created, but instead ask them to tell me about it.

Actually, almost all of the suggestions given for adults earlier in this chapter can be adjusted to also work well for children. It is good, for example, for children to be a part of the funeral planning, the sharing of stories, and all the rituals of memory and grief. Working with a child to create a memory book, or doing something loving in honor of one who died can be healing for both the child and the one working with the child.

Children are often the forgotten mourners. It is so important to remember that children grieve, and to provide them the safety of our love in a world that has also changed dramatically for them. As children come to understand the painful truth that their loved one is not coming back, we can help them to also know the good news: that *love is forever!* Though our loved one is gone from our sight, he or she is not gone from our hearts. The person who loved us in life still loves us in death; and we still love him or her. That is forever.

There is also much that we can learn from our children.

When the grandmother of a young boy named Paul died, he thought about his grandma's death and everything he had heard his family say about it. Paul decided to write God a letter. The letter he wrote to God was very simple. It was wise in a way that often only a child can be. He wrote:

> *Dear God,*
> *My grandma just died. Please take care of her,*
> *and give her a hug for me. You'll know who she is.*
> *Her name is "Grandma."*
>
> > *Signed,*
> > *Your friend,*
> > *Paul*

I'm sure God did just that.

"Blessed are they who mourn . . ."–Jesus
—Matthew 5:4

57

WE ARE GOD'S RESPONSE

*Above all in times of darkness, that is the time
to love—that an act of love may tip the balance.*

—Elie Wiesel

As a little girl prepared for bed one night, she was getting more and more worried about an approaching storm she heard in the distance. When she said goodnight to her mom and dad, she told them she was afraid. Mom and dad told her that she didn't have to worry. "God will be right there with you," they said. She did not seem completely convinced. She went upstairs to bed, but the thunder got louder and louder so she called downstairs, "I'm scared!" Her mom and dad said, "You don't have to be afraid; God is right there with you." She looked around her room but didn't see God there. Suddenly there was a bright flash of lightning and a huge clap of thunder and she called out, "Well, I need a God with skin on!"

Perhaps that is a good description of our role as Christians: by how we live and love, we are to put *skin* on God. We tell those who suffer that "God is with them," and rightly so. Yet, how will most people know that God is with them except that they experience that presence through our care, our reaching out to them?

In addition to the sufferings that are thrust upon us by life, there is another suffering, one that is called from us by our Baptism: the freely chosen suffering of love. This is the call of all who choose to live the way of Jesus.

Perhaps when we see people who are hurting and who cry out to God, "Why don't you do something about this?" if we could hear God's answer, we would hear God say, "I did: I created *you*."

"Putting Skin On" God

A little boy was sitting at his desk in his second-grade classroom when suddenly he was aware of a puddle between his feet, and that the front of his pants was wet. He could not imagine how this happened. It had never happened before. The poor little guy was so embarrassed that he wanted to die. He was sure that when the guys found out, he'd never hear the end of it and that the girls in the class would never speak to him again.

"Please, dear God," he prayed, "I'm in big trouble. I need help!"

He looked up from his prayer to see a classmate named Susie carrying a gold fish bowl filled with water. Suddenly she lost her grip on the bowl and dumped the water right into the boy's lap. The boy pretended to be angry—but he was praying, "Thank you, Jesus! Thank you, Jesus!" Now, instead of being the object of ridicule, the boy received sympathy. The teacher rushed him downstairs and gave him gym shorts to put on while his pants dried. All the children were on their hands and knees cleaning up the mess.

Now poor Susie was the one considered the "klutz." She tried to help, but they told her to get away, angry at her for doing such a dumb thing. So it went for the rest of the day: He was surrounded by sympathy while poor Susie was shunned.

After school, the two were waiting for the bus. Susie was standing off by herself. He walked up to her and whispered, "You did that on purpose, didn't you?"

Susie whispered back, "I wet my pants once, too."

In what she did, Susie *put skin on* God for that young boy. For, indeed, that is the kind of God that we have . . . the God who reaches out to us in our suffering, embracing our every pain and humiliation.

Presence

It is our calling that we put *skin* on God for those who suffer, and we do that best by our *presence;* by our willingness to be with others in their suffering. Being present to someone in their struggles does not necessarily mean that we try to fix them or the situation. It means that we listen to their pain, and walk with them during the difficult times. Presence is the most important gift we can give.

A teenage boy underwent chemotherapy for cancer. The result of chemotherapy was that he lost his hair. When it was time for him to return to school, he and his family tried wigs, hats, bandannas, and various ways to try to make him not stand out and feel embarrassed in front of his classmates. They finally settled on a baseball cap. When he left for school that day, he was still embarrassed, and hoped that no one would make fun of him. What did he find when he got to school? He found that all of his friends had shaved their heads, too. They wanted him to know that he was not alone.

One of the greatest mistakes we make with those who are hurting is that often we do nothing. Maybe we are not sure what to say. Perhaps we avoid them because it is hard to be around another's pain while not being able to make everything okay. Unfortunately, then, when people are most in need, they are often left most alone.

The poem: *"The Elephant In The Room,"* by Terry Kettering describes well the loneliness caused by our tendency to avoid people in their sadness:

> *There's an elephant in the room.*
> *It is large and squatting, so it is hard to get around it.*
> *Yet we squeeze by with "How are you?" and "I'm fine."*
> *And a thousand other forms of trivial chatter.*
> *We talk about the weather.*
> *We talk about work.*
> *We talk about everything else—except the elephant in the room.*
> *There's an elephant in the room.*
> *We all know it is there.*
> *We are thinking about the elephant as we talk together.*
> *It is constantly on our minds.*

For, you see, it is a very big elephant.
It has hurt us all.
But we do not talk about the elephant in the room.
Oh, please, say her name.
Oh, please, say "Barbara" again.
Oh, please, let's talk about the elephant in the room.
For if we talk about her death,
Perhaps we can talk about her life.
Can I say "Barbara" to you and not have you look away?
For if I cannot, then you are leaving me
Alone . . . In a room . . .
With an elephant.

Terry Kettering, "The Elephant in the Room,"
(Colorado Springs, Colo: Bereavement Publishing Inc.).

What Do We Say? The Danger of Words

Certainly it is important that we reach out to those who have lost a loved one to death. Whatever a person's manner of grieving, we do well to reach out to them by calling, writing, or making time to be with them.

It's important, however, to give some thought to what we really want to say to those who have had a loss. Perhaps it is because we are uncomfortable that we feel we need to say something. Unfortunately, though, sometimes what we say is not helpful at all. It is *not* a good idea to say such things as: "Don't cry," or "I'm sure that God did this for a good reason," or "I know exactly how you feel."

Usually the best thing is to simply say, "I'm sorry," and then to be quiet, maybe hold the person's hand, and listen. When a person says, "Why me?" or "Why would God let this happen to such a good person?" they do not need answers. They simply need their pain to be heard. At times like this, it is usually best to say, "I'm sorry. It's really hard, isn't it?" or "Tell me what it's like for you." Then listen.

One woman who was having a hard day had a husband who was sensitive to this but didn't know what to say. When he asked about it she told him, "You can put your arm around me, tell me you love me, and try not to say anything cheerful." Such an approach is usually the most helpful.

If we do not personally know the deceased, it is often good to ask the grieving to tell us about their loved one and what he or she was like. Also, it is good to remember that holidays, birthdays, and anniversaries can be intensely painful for years for those who have lost loved ones. It can be a real blessing for those who are grieving if we tell them we are aware that they are spending this occasion without their loved one and let them know we are wondering how they are doing. When we do this, we need to communicate an openness to hearing how they really are, aware that there is likely a mixture of emotions and reactions. Often, they will want to talk. If they do not, that is fine. We simply tell them that we are thinking about them, while being careful not to push them just to fulfill our own need to be helpful.

When we call or offer help, we often say, "Please let me know if there is anything I can do." That approach, though well intentioned, might not be effective. Most people will not be able to ask for help in response to such a statement. Instead, it is much better if we first listen to our own hearts about what we want to offer, and then offer that. Perhaps we could offer to sit with them at the doctor's office; maybe provide transportation for their children to and from school; perhaps help with correspondence or yard work. One woman I know knocked on her neighbor's door with a bucket and a mop in hand and said, "I'd love to wash your kitchen and bathroom floors, if you wouldn't mind." Such specific offers are much more likely to be accepted.

Similarly, regarding prayer, instead of simply telling someone we will pray for them, it is often good to pray right then and there. Perhaps in some cases we could say, "Yes, I will indeed keep you in my prayers. How about if we take a moment of prayer together right now?" Then, whether face-to-face, or on the phone, pray for a moment with the person.

All too often people try to "be strong" for each other. This is not the way of Christ. We do ourselves—and each other—a great disservice by deciding we should carry our struggles all by ourselves. God gave us each other so that we would not have to go it alone! Let us speak honestly with one another, and when we're sad, let us cry together.

I hold up, as a good example, a little girl who one day came home late from school. Her mother was worried, "Where were you? Why were you late?" The little girl explained, "On the way home I saw Jamie who was sad and crying, so

I helped her." "What did you do to help her?" her mom asked. She answered, "I sat down and cried with her."

We cannot understand, nor take away another's pain. And yes, we do need to take care of ourselves when caring for others. But, it is clearly our call as followers of Christ to stretch ourselves to be with those who suffer, to sit with one another in times of pain or loss.

The Gift of a Small Kindness

Certainly we could never heal the many sufferings and injustices of this world. Often it feels as if we have so little to offer, but it is essential that we do reach out to do what we can. Though it may seem that we don't have much to offer, God takes our little part and works great beauty from it. A small act of kindness can mean so much!

Once a woman brought her young child to see a concert by the great pianist Ignace Paderewski. Before the concert, she was talking to a friend sitting next to her and didn't notice until the lights began to dim that her son had slipped away. She anxiously looked around for him, and as the curtains opened and stage lights went up, she saw to her horror that her son was sitting at the concert piano plunking out the tune "Twinkle, Twinkle, Little Star." At that very moment, Paderewski came out to begin, saw the child, and realized what was happening. He slipped in behind the young boy and whispered, "Keep playing." As the little boy played the tune "Twinkle, Twinkle, Little Star" with one finger, Paderewski put his hands on either side and began to fill in a wonderful accompaniment, to the delight of the entire crowd.

So it is with our efforts to reach out to those who are hurting in any way. We offer our simple bit of help, and God, the master musician, fills in around us to make something wonderful from our simple efforts.

In fact, the love in our hearts for another who is in need is not only what God is like—it actually *is* God. Though we cannot fix people or end their suffering by our willingness to reach out to them and to be with them in their pain, we do indeed "put skin on" God, the God who is with us in our suffering . . . the God who brings life from death.

Indeed it is true that when we face the suffering of the world, we stand before great mystery. But we do not stand alone, without hope, or without something to offer. By how we love one another we help make real the promise that, no matter what we suffer, on the other end of our suffering, God will catch us in the arms of love

Above all in times of darkness, that is the time to love—that an act of love may tip the balance.
—Elie Wiesel

PART THREE

Before I formed you in the womb
I knew you.—God

(Jeremiah 1:4)

Introduction

Shortly after I'd completed the children's version of the video *No One Cries the Wrong Way,* a teacher at a nearby school called the rectory to inquire how she might obtain a copy of the video for her class. Our secretary, unaware of the video and its actual name, left me a note that someone was looking for a copy of the new video, *Knowing Christ the Wrong Way.*

Though I chuckled, the phrase stayed with me. Is there such a thing as knowing Christ the wrong way? Certainly getting to know Jesus is made less attractive—and even difficult—by some of the distorted ways Christianity is presented. It is clear to me that once we have truly met Jesus, then we know him rightly, and as he is: Beautiful . . . humble . . . challenging . . . courageous . . . self-emptying . . . real . . . with us always.

For too long I was convinced that I was inadequate to the task of knowing Christ. It seemed to me that others had a wonderful relationship with God . . . but not I. Maybe I just didn't know how; perhaps I wasn't good enough. Yet, by God's marvelous initiative I have now come to realize that I don't have the power to *keep* God from loving me. Maybe I'm not as smart as the person next to me, but God is so wonderful that God knows how to find me anyway. I see now that God is *omni-lingual:* God knows how to communicate in a way that even I understand. In truth, whatever our language, personality, history, or way of life, God knows how to reach each of us intimately in a way that is as real and unique as we are.

That is, in part, why it is good to take some time alone, and if possible, with others, to use the quotes, questions, prayers, and activities in this part of the book. Reflection on our life-experiences can help us be more aware of the ways that God does speak in our lives . . . and help us to actually *know* Christ.

Clearly, the questions around the mystery of suffering are difficult and often gutwrenching, but as I said earlier, I believe that it is extremely important that we wrestle with them. For in the end, they lead us to love.

THE QUESTION

Questions for Personal Reflection or Group Discussion

Given all that is painful in the world, what gives you hope?

Louis Pasteur said, "I do not ask your religion or your opinion, only what is your suffering?" How would you answer that question: What is your suffering?

Crosses and crucifixes are present in almost every Catholic institution. One reason for the presence of the crucifixes is to indicate that this is a place where we find meaning in suffering. What is your reaction when you look at a cross or crucifix?

Suggested Activities

For prayer, take a globe in your hands (or something that can symbolize the world for you), put music on in the background, and without words hold it to God in prayer, moving with it as you feel drawn.

Try "praying the news." Take a moment of prayer before you turn on the news, and ask God to help you react as God would in response to the news: to be sad where God would be sad, angry at those things that God sees as unjust, and grateful for that which brings life. Then listen to the news with God's heart, offering a prayer in response to each segment.

At the end of the day, look back and list some of the ways love was present for you during the day.

Chapter One

Quotes for Meditation and Prayer

"History is not fixed. It does not move inevitably toward either perfection or destruction . . . history has a capacity for being changed from within." —Douglas John Hall

"And Jesus wept." —John 11:35

"We must let go of God in order to find God." —Meister Eckhart

"A ship is safe in the harbor, but that is not what a ship is for." —Thomas Aquinas

Prayer Service: "Cup of Sorrow . . . Cup of Joy"

Please note that each prayer service can be modified to be prayed by an individual or by groups of various sizes. Please make whatever adjustments you find helpful.

Materials needed:
- a large goblet or cup
- small pieces of paper
- pencils
- a Bible

Each person takes two pieces of paper. Participants are asked to jot down one or more of their life's greatest "sorrows" on one piece, and on the other, to write one or more of their life's greatest "joys."

Reading: John 11:32–36

(Play reflective music softly in the background throughout this service. One possible suggestion for reflective music is Stephen Petrunak's "With Hope and Healing" available from GIA Publications, Inc. 1-800-442-1358, www.giamusic.com)

The leader puts his or her own slip of paper into the cup, passes the cup, and says in these or similar words: **"As we pass the cup this first time, we invite you to place into it the paper which names some of your joys. It is good that we remember our blessings. As we do so, let us remember that Jesus, too, embraced human joy. By entering fully into our humanity, Jesus also came to know the blessings and delights of life."**

(When the cup returns to the leader, the leader holds it high in prayer): "Jesus, we lift to you this cup which holds some of that which brings us joy. You, too, knew laughter and love. You, too, delighted in that which was good. As we lift this cup, we say 'thank you.' Thank you for all that brings joy and delight into our world. Help us keep grateful hearts."

(The leader lowers the cup, asks participants to take the paper with their "sorrows," and to symbolically make a tear in the paper to depict the brokenness that comes with our pain). The participants put the torn slips of paper in the cup as it is passed again. As they do this , the leader says: "As we place our sorrows into this cup, let us remember that Jesus embraced our every sorrow and pain, . . . even our death."

(When the cup returns to the leader, the leader raises the cup high): "Jesus, we lift to you this cup, mixed with our sorrows and our joys. You drank deeply of human joy . . . and also of our suffering and pain. Help us, as you did, to drink deeply of life's sweetness and its sorrow. May we know that you are in them with us. You laugh with us, you cry with us. You live with us, you die with us. Help us to come to know that you are with us always."

The leader invites all to join hands, and says: "Remembering our solidarity with all those who suffer, let us end by praying together the Lord's Prayer."

Personal Reflection Journal

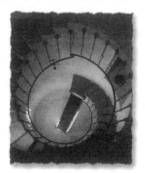

THE ANSWERER

Questions for Personal Reflection or Group Discussion

What qualities of God are most appealing to you?

"Until you have cried, you do not know God" (Saint Ephraem). Is it possible that our tears could be *holy water,* having the potential to help us know God? In what pain or suffering in your life have you known this?

Latin American theologian Juan Luis Segundo says, "The world should not be the way it is." How *should* the world be?

Has there ever been a suffering in your life such that when you look back on it now, you see that God was with you, holding you close? How did God do that for you?

Suggested Activities

Hold a crucifix in your hands and let it help you imagine the crucifixion scene. Picture Jesus weeping on the cross. As you see him there, say whatever you feel like saying to him.

Take clay (or some other material) and form an image that shows something of God's relationship with you. You might keep this, repeat the activity several months later, and then compare the two images.

Plan how you might "tithe your time with those who are poor," spending time with those who wear their brokenness "on the outside": persons with disabilities, persons who are in care centers, the hungry at soup kitchens, and so on. What might this teach you of your own brokenness? What might you see of God?

Chapter Two

Quotes for Meditation and Prayer

"To say, "God is love," is the least wrong thing we could say about God." —Michael Himes

"Peace . . . is not the absence of struggle . . . it is knowing we are not alone in it." —Pat Livingston

"And know that I am with you always, until the end of the world!" —Jesus (Matthew 28:20)

"Christ gives the answer to the question about suffering and the meaning of suffering not only by his teaching . . . but most of all by his own suffering . . . " —Pope John Paul II in *Salvifici Doloris*

Prayer Service: Love Crucified

Materials needed:
- crucifix (more than one for a larger group)
- papers
- pencil

Each participant is invited to get in touch with a loss or suffering that is real for them. If it is helpful, perhaps participants can take a minute or two to write a few words to describe their loss, or to draw a picture of the suffering.

(Play reflective music softly in the background throughout this service.)

The leader then says in these or similar words: **"The cross is the most powerful statement of the love of God: that God's own Son embraced our every suffering, even our death. As we pass the crucifix from person to person, I ask you to hold the crucifix for 15 to 20 seconds, looking at the face of Jesus. Whatever words are in your heart, offer them silently. Or simply gaze at the face of Christ with no words, and know that you are loved."**

The leader then invites everyone to repeat after each statement the following response: *You are always with us.*

On our life's journey, we never walk alone,

In times of joy, laughter, and health,

In times of uncertainty, fear, and doubt,

In times of sadness, loss, illness, and death,

No matter where we go or what we do,

Closing Prayer

God our father, God of all compassion, you love us more than we could ever imagine. You have embraced our pain and suffering, and so we, your children, do not suffer alone. As we bring to you the broken places of our own lives and of our world, we pray that you will bring life from death, hope from sorrow, meaning in loss. Help us to remember, God our loving father, that you are, indeed, with us always. We pray through Christ, our Lord. Amen.

Personal Reflection Journal

THE MORE
IMPORTANT QUESTION

Questions for Personal Reflection or Group Discussion

Have you been transformed by a suffering? What parts of it do you value now? If there were a magic pill that could change you physically, emotionally, and spiritually to the way you were before your suffering, would you take it?

In the Vietnamese and Chinese languages, the word crisis is actually translated into two words: *danger* and *opportunity.* Describe a struggle in your life where you see both danger and opportunity.

The question "Why?" ultimately needs to yield to the question, "Now what?" Now how do I live? Describe a difficult situation in your life and write an answer for the question, "Now what?"

Describe a time when a decision you made felt like a leap of faith. How was God there to catch you?

Suggested Activities

Turn to Philippians 2:6–11, Paul's great hymn to self-emptying love. Think of someone you know whose attitude was "that of Christ," who emptied themselves for love. How has God, because of this, raised that person to new life?

Designate a notebook or binder as a "gratitude journal." At the end of each day, list three new things that you are grateful for.

Chapter Three

Quotes for Meditation and Prayer

"He did not say: You will not be troubled, you will not be belabored, you will not be afflicted; but he said: You will not be overcome."
—Julian of Norwich

"If you get rid of the pain before you have answered its question, you get rid of the self along with it." —Carl Jung

"All is changed, changed utterly. A terrible beauty is born." —W.B. Yeats

"It is suffering more than anything else, which clears the way for the grace which transforms human souls." —Pope John Paul II

"It ain't over 'till it's over." —Yogi Berra

God, grant me the serenity to accept the things I cannot change, the courage to change the things I can, and the wisdom to know the difference.—Reinhold Niebuhr

Prayer Service: Life from the Shattered Pieces

Materials needed:
- box of new crayons (enough for each person to have at least one)
- sheets of paper (at least one for each participant)

Each person is given a sheet of paper and asked to choose a crayon.

Leader prays,

God, grant me the serenity to accept the things I cannot change, the courage to change the things I can, and the wisdom to know the difference.

Each person is asked to use his or her crayon to draw a picture or a symbol of pain or brokenness . . . (for example: a cross, a teardrop, a broken heart, and so on).

Everyone is then invited to break their crayon in half, and to draw with their *broken* crayon a picture or symbol of hope, healing, or happiness.

Closing Prayer

Lord, we know we will be forever changed by our brokenness. Help us to remember that there is life even in the midst of that which is broken and painful. Color our lives with hope. We pray through Christ our Lord.

The leader invites all to stand and to end the prayer service by offering and receiving a sign of peace.

Personal Reflection Journal

WHY PRAY?

Questions for Personal Reflection or Group Discussion

Pope John Paul I said that God is not only father, but also mother. If you were to write a letter to God as mother, what would you say?

How do you pray? What helps you?

Reflect on a time when you looked for God. What happened? Reflect on a time when you were aware of God looking for you. Where were you hiding?

Talk about a time, this day or this week, when you were aware of God's presence.

Suggested Activities

Designate a small table or part of your dresser as a "prayer table." Each week, place an item or reminder on it that helps open you toward God.

Choose an adjective from list A that describes your relationship with God, then a word from list B which you would use to address God. Write a short letter or prayer to God using the words you have chosen (for example, "Merciful Savior . . . ")

Chapter Four

List A

Merciful	Gentle	Silent	Compassionate
Loving	Awesome	Surprising	_____
Distant	Tender	Holy	*(other personal*
Almighty	Fearsome	Humble	*choice)*

List B

Friend	Sister	God	Sanctifier
Lover	Father	Brother	Savior
Redeemer	Creator	Hope	_____
Lord	Companion	Mother	*(other personal*
Spirit	Son	Life	*choice)*

Pray one phrase of the Lord's Prayer each day this week, reflecting on that phrase throughout the whole day.

Go to a beautiful place. Then, with your eyes closed, open each of your senses one at a time: first smell, then taste, then touch, then hearing, and only then, while aware of each of the other senses, also open your eyes. With or without words, whisper a prayer.

Quotes for Meditation and Prayer

"God is at home. It is we who have gone out for a walk."
—Meister Eckhart

"Joy is the most infallible sign of the presence of God."—Leon Bloy

"Dear God, is it ok to talk to you even when I don't want anything?"
Love, Eric
—Children's Letters to God

"Be still, and know that I am God." God —(Psalm 46:10a)

Listen! I am standing at the door, knocking; if you hear my voice and open the door, I will come in to you and eat with you, and you with me. Jesus —(Revelation 3:20)

Prayer Service: Be Still

The leader should explain to the participants that he or she will be reading five phrases. After each phrase there will be a ten second pause *(Note: It is critical for the leader to pause in order to realize the full effect.)*. The leader invites participants to close their eyes

Be still and know that I am God   (pause)

Be still and know that I am   (pause)

Be still and know   (pause)

Be still   (pause)

Be   (pause)

To complete the prayer service, ask the participants to open their eyes and repeat these lines of prayer from Dag Hammerskjold.

Leader:	For all that has been,
All:	For all that has been,
Leader:	thank you.
All:	thank you.
Leader:	For all that will be,
All:	For all that will be,
Leader:	yes.
All:	yes.

Personal Reflection Journal

DIGNITY IN LIFE AND IN DEATH

Questions for Personal Reflection or Group Discussion

Much of our culture falsely teaches that our dignity is to be found on the outside. Rate, on a scale from one to ten, which of the following expressions of that untruth are you likely to believe?

- Clothes make the person; looks are very important.
- Financial security gives peace.
- I must earn love by *doing.*
- I can never live down my past mistakes.
- If I don't have my health, I don't have anything.
- What others think of me is essential.
- Other _____.

How are you affected by such thinking, and what helps you counteract this message?

A Buddhist tradition encourages followers to imagine every day that there is a little bird on their shoulder who asks, "Is today the day I die?" What would you do differently if you knew that you only had a short time to live?

What do you fear most about dying?

Mohammed said, "You must die before you die." What experiences of "letting go" at this time of your life do you think will help you let go at the end of your life in this world?

If you received news from the doctor that you were soon to die, whom would you tell? What would you want to say to him or her?

Describe someone you know who "died well."

Suggested Activities

To help clarify what is important in our lives, it can be good to write an obituary for ourselves. Fill in the appropriate blanks below, and use extra space as needed:

_____ died today at age _____.
He or she is survived by _____
and will be remembered by _____.
Mr./Ms. _____ was noted for
_____. His or her significant
accomplishments have been _____.
At the time of death he or she was actively involved in _____
_____. He or she would like to
be remembered as _____.

Encourage an aged relative or friend to write or make a tape of some of their favorite memories, perhaps including a "final message."

Sign your organ donation card, and inform your family of your wishes. Pursue making advance care directives and filling out a living will.

Think of a loved one who is aged or ill and write down what you would like to be sure to say to him or her while you have the chance. Include telling the person what you are sorry for, grateful about, and that you forgive and love him or her. If possible, visit this loved one and tell him or her in person what you want to say.

Quotes for Meditation and Prayer

"Do not seek death. Death will find you. But seek the road which makes death a fulfillment." —Dag Hammarskjold

"We need, in love, to practice only this: letting each other go. For holding on comes easily; we do not need to learn it." —Rainer Maria Rilke

"Sartre was right: You have to live each moment as if you're prepared to die." —Anatole Broyard

"It might be more helpful if people would talk about death and dying as an intrinsic part of life just as they do not hesitate to mention when someone is having a baby." —Elizabeth Kübler Ross

"Before I formed you in the womb I knew you . . ."—Jeremiah 1:4

Prayer Service: Lay Our Hands

Leader using these or similar words:

When people are sick, they often lack physical and emotional connection with the community. Many people who are homebound or in a home for those who are elderly report that one of the things they miss most is others physically touching them. In the Sacrament of the Anointing of the Sick, the person is touched as he or she is anointed with oil. The priest lays hands on the head of the one who is sick and prays for him or her with the Church's love.

We, too, will pray for each other now, utilizing the healing touch of Christ. In just a moment, I will ask you to turn to one another and take turns "laying hands" on the other person—on their heads, shoulders, and so on,—as you are comfortable. You will be praying silently for the other's deepest need. There is no "formula" in this prayer. Perhaps you will have words in your heart as you pray silently, or perhaps you will simply let the love of God flow through you without words. After one person has been prayed for, alternate so that the person just prayed for now prays over the other person in a similar manner. Remember to take your time with this . . . pray silently for each other for about 20 or 30 seconds.

(The leader plays meditative music softly as the "laying on of hands" begins.)

When the laying on of hands is concluded, the leader invites all to pray together:

"Glory be to the Father, and to the Son, and to the Holy Spirit. As it was in the beginning, is now, and will be forever. Amen."

Personal Reflection Journal

Life Beyond Life

Questions for Personal Reflection or Group Discussion

If you had a chance to say something to a loved one who has died, whom would you pick, and what would you say?

Sometimes in our ordinary daily living we get *promissory experiences* of heaven, tastes of the eternal now. Discuss an experience from your life that gives a glimpse of the beauty of heaven.

Who is in heaven rooting for you?

If you knew that a family member or someone you love would soon die, what would you do?

Describe one of your loved ones who has died and what you appreciated about him or her.

Suggested Activities

Invite family members, your church group, or some friends to write a eulogy for one another. Divide the names among the group, then have each person write a eulogy for another, and share it with the group.

Chapter Six

Participants may choose their own format or use the following form:

Today we gather to pay tribute to _____. He or she is

remembered and honored today for _____.

If we could, we would thank him or her for _____;

tell him or her we are sorry for _____;

and ask him or her to pray for us that _____.

We will miss her or him, especially because _____.

Imagine that you received news from the doctor that you had only three more months to live. Whom would you tell first? Write a letter to tell him or her what you would want to say to him or her before you die.

Plan parts of your own funeral: What songs would you like? What Scripture readings? What message would you want to be preached? Who would you want to be pallbearers, and so on?

Quotes for Meditation and Prayer

"There is a land of the living and a land of the dead and the bridge is love, the only survival, the only meaning." —Thornton Wilder

"Out of the finite darkness, into the infinite light."
—Louise Chandler Moulton

"And when the earth shall claim your limbs, then shall you truly dance." —Kahlil Gibran

"Life is eternal; and love is immortal; and death is only a horizon; and a horizon is nothing save the limit of our sight"
—Rossiter W. Raymond

I know that my redeemer lives. —Job 19:25 [NRSV]

Prayer Service: Welcome them Home

Materials needed:
- bowl of water
- candle
- matches
- instrumental music

(Begin playing instrumental music softly in the background.) The leader holds up a bowl of water and prays: "**God of all life, at the very dawn of creation your Spirit hovered over the waters to bring order from chaos. Through the waters of the Red Sea you led your people out of slavery into freedom. In the waters of Baptism you plunged us into the death of Christ that we might rise with him to new life forever. Bless this water, and lead us more deeply into you.**"

After the blessing, the leader invites each participant to come forward, dip a hand into the water, make a sign of the cross, and then gather into a circle.

After all are in place, the leader takes the lighted candle, holds it up, and prays: "**On the day of our baptism, we were handed a candle that was lighted from the Paschal candle. The light of Christ that was given to us shines on in darkness, even in death. We will now pass the candle to each person gathered here. As you hold the candle, speak the name of a loved one who has died, or if you prefer, remember them in silence, and then pass the candle to the person next to you.**" The leader begins by saying the name of a loved one who has died, then passes the candle to the next person until all have finished.

Closing Prayer

Jesus, we bring to you in prayer our loved ones who have died. We ask you to welcome them home, put loving arms around them, give them a hug for us, and fill them with peace. As we walk this earth without their physical presence, may we draw strength and comfort from your love. We ask this in your name. Amen.

Personal Reflection Journal

TO GRIEVE

Questions for Personal Reflection or Group Discussion

Whom or what are you grieving at this time in your life? What emotions are the strongest now?

When someone we love dies, we often ask, "Why did they die?" There is another question, "Why did they live?" We did not deserve their death, nor did we deserve their life. Write or talk about the gift of the life of someone you know who has died.

Though we do not believe that God causes evil in order to bring good out of it, often we can see that good has come from a death or loss. Describe any good that you have seen resulting from the death of a loved one.

Many find it difficult to receive help. How can people offer help to you in a way that makes it easier for you to receive?

Suggested Activities

Have a family "remembrance" evening and share stories, photographs, and memories of the loved one who has died. Perhaps participate in an activity that the person loved to do.

Often it can be good to write an honest, uncensored letter to a loved one who has died. Use the following sentence starters and write a letter to your loved one. (Perhaps let each line below be the beginning of a separate letter).

My Dear _____,
I want to tell you some of the things that I miss about you . . .
I'm sorry for . . .
Some of the wonderful things others have said about you since your death . . .
I'm so angry about . . .
What I feel guilty about these days is . . .
I forgive you for . . .
I thank you for . . .
What's hardest for me now is . . .
Please pray for me that . . . .

On birthdays, holidays, or anniversaries buy your loved one a gift and donate it to a nursing home, homeless shelter, or other group that would benefit from it.

For someone who died of AIDS, make a quilt for the Names Project Quilt, 310 Townsend St., San Francisco, CA 94107.

Plant a young tree or flowering plant in your loved one's name.

Keep a journal of your memories — your loved one's life, their dying, the funeral, the days after, and so on.

Quotes for Meditation and Prayer

"It is such a secret place, the land of tears."—Antoine de Saint-Exupery

"And Jesus wept. 'See how he loved him.'"—John 11:35–36

"I cannot say what loves have come and gone; I only know that summer sang in me a little while, that in me sings no more."
—Edna Saint Vincent Millay

"A man (sic) no longer what he was, nor yet the thing he'd planned . . . I think you will have need of tears." —Edna Saint Vincent Millay

"Some survivors try to think their way through grief. That doesn't work. Grief is a releasing process, a discovery process, a healing process . . . The brain must follow the heart at a respectful distance."
—Carol Staudacher

"I picked up the fragments of my life and put them together, all but the missing piece." —Kamala Markandaya

"If you can't feel your pain, you're not going to feel anything else either." —Berger to Conrad in *Ordinary People*

Prayer Service: We Remember

For this prayer service, invite each participant to bring something that symbolizes the life of, or something that was important to a person he or she loved who died (for example, a baseball hat, Bible, photo, serving spoon, and so on)

Materials needed:

- a white cloth draped over a prayer table (to symbolize a pall)
- lit candle
- a Bible
- instrumental music
- the symbols brought by participants

Choose someone to be the reader.

The leader says: **"In the revised funeral Mass, family or friends are welcome to place on the coffin a gift symbolic of the deceased person's faith. At this time, we invite you to bring up, one at a time, a symbol of your loved one, to hold it up to the group, and if you would like, to say a brief word about why you chose it. Then place it on or near the prayer table. If anyone forgot or was unable to bring an object, you can describe it."**

When this is concluded, the reader proclaims the following reading from *Isaiah 49:14–16:*

> But Zion said, "The Lord has forsaken me;
> my Lord has forgotten me."
> Can a mother forget her infant,
> be without tenderness for the child of her womb?
> Even should she forget,
> I will never forget you.
> See, upon the palms of my hands I have written your name.
> The Word of the Lord.

The leader continues: "Let us pray. God of all tenderness, we commend to your merciful care our loved ones who have died. We thank you for blessing the world with their lives. We thank you for all that brought them joy. We choose to trust that, true to your word, you have not forgotten them. Nor have you forgotten us in our loss. Help us, in their name, to choose again this day to love and to live well the remaining days we have on this earth. We pray through Christ our Lord.

Let us close by sharing a sign of Christ's peace with one another.

Personal Reflection Journal

WE ARE GOD'S RESPONSE

Questions for Personal Reflection or Group Discussion

Discuss a time when you were a loving presence for someone else. What were some of the costs to you? What were some of the gifts you received in the process?

Edmund Burke said, "All that is necessary for evil to triumph is for good people to do nothing." What is one good you could have done that you regret you did not do?

The poem, "The Elephant in the Room" describes the loneliness of having a loss that no one talks about. Was there ever an elephant in your room? Describe.

Dietrich Bonhoeffer distinguishes "general suffering" and "Christian suffering," the latter earmarked by being voluntary, bearing the burdens of others, and being done for the sake of Christ. Describe someone you know who lives "Christian suffering."

In any experience of suffering in your life, was there anyone or anything that helped you know that Jesus was with you? Explain.

Suggested Activities

Think of those you know who have had a loved one die or have experienced another loss. Put their names and special dates on a calendar to remind yourself to call or to write them.

Pray for the grace at the beginning of the day to see someone who gets picked on, is ignored, or is suffering in any way, and to be ready to offer them an extra kind word.

Insert into the Beatitudes *(Matthew 5:3–12)* the names of people you know who live them: *(for example, "Blessed is John who is poor in spirit. He has found joy in serving the homeless. Blessed is Brenda who brings peace by . . . and so on.)*

Quotes for Meditation and Prayer

"Whatever God does, the first outburst is always compassion." —Eckhart

"Concern for those in severe need is not a matter of choice for the Christian; it is to be a Christian." —Diogenes Allen

"Apathy might not be the most dramatic form of suicide, just the most common." —William J. O'Malley

"We have much more to offer than we may realize. All we have to do is ask, "How can I help?" with an open heart, and then really listen." —Ram Dass and Paul Gorman

"Come, you who are blessed by my Father. Inherit the kingdom prepared for you from the foundation of the world. For I was hungry and you gave me food, I was thirsty and you gave me drink, a stranger and you welcomed me, naked and you clothed me, ill and you cared for me, in prison and you visited me." —Jesus (Matthew 25:34–36)

Prayer Service: The Light of Christ

Materials needed:
- three candles
- candle holder
- matches
- hymnals (if prayer of Saint Francis is to be sung)

The leader begins by saying, "Let's take a moment for each of us to think of some of the people we know who make God real for us, and some of the ways they do that." (pause)

"We will now offer, in thanksgiving, the names of some of those who have been there for us in our need." The leader begins, saying for example, "**For my friend, Carolyn.**"

When all have had a chance to speak, the leader lights the first candle and prays, "**God of all light and goodness, we thank you for the people who bring your light to our world by their care. For their kindness, their laughter, their faith, and their goodness, we thank you through Christ our Lord.**" (Leader places a lit candle in a holder on the table.)

"**We will now pray for some of our own needs.**" The leader begins, saying for example, "For peace in my home."

When all have had a chance to pray, the leader lights the second candle and prays,: "**God of all compassion, we hold to you our needs. Fill the darkness in our world with the light of your peace. Fill the darkness in our homes with the light of your forgiveness. Fill the darkness in our hearts with the light of your love. We pray through Christ our Lord. Amen.** (Leader places a lit candle in a holder on the table.)

"**We will now pray for some of those who need us, and for whom we are called to reach out to in love.**" The leader begins, saying for example: "For my co-worker who recently lost her husband."

When all have had a chance to pray, the leader holds the third candle *unlit* and prays: "**God of all compassion, we hold this unlit candle that we might remember those who need the light of your love. Though we are weak and sinful, you count on us to bring your light to others. As we go from here, help us to be aware of those who suffer. By how we love them, may they know that you are with them. We pray through Christ our Lord. Amen.**" (Leader places unlit candle in a holder on the table.)

The prayer service is concluded by singing or praying together the Prayer of Saint Francis.

Prayer of Saint Francis

Lord, make me an instrument of your peace.
Where there is hatred, let me sow love.
Where there is injury, pardon.
Where there is doubt, faith.
Where there is despair, hope.
Where there is darkness, light.
Where there is sadness, joy.

O Master, grant that I may not so much seek to be consoled as to console.
To be understood as to understand. To be loved as to love.
For it is in giving that we receive. It is in pardoning that we are pardoned, and it is in dying that we are born to eternal life. Amen.

Personal Reflection Journal

FACE-TO-FACE WITH JESUS
AN EXPERIENCE OF GUIDED PRAYER

Shortly before I was ordained a priest, I went on retreat with my classmates. After each of the retreat presentations, we were expected to go to our rooms for an hour of prayer. I remember how strongly I felt then that I really didn't know how to pray. Though I tried to do everything as I had been taught, I could not escape the feeling that I was completely inadequate to the task. While I imagined my classmates having wonderful encounters with God, it seemed to me that I didn't know how to do anything else but talk to myself in the darkness. I remember thinking that it would be great if Jesus would just walk into the room, and he and I could sit down face-to-face to talk things through. It would seem to be so much easier than talking to emptiness.

As I continued to think about that, I wondered what would I do if Jesus actually *did* walk into my room to be with me? That question so intrigued me that I spent the next several minutes imagining just that. What were the things for which I would want to tell Jesus "Thanks"? For what would I want to tell him I was sorry? What concerns would I bring him to ask his help with?

After spending some time thinking about what I would do if Jesus actually did come into my room, I then went ahead and used my imagination to picture that encounter. I imaged Jesus sitting with me face-to-face. I poured out to Jesus what was in my heart. It was for me a very good way to pray.

In this exercise I invite you to a similar experience of prayer. In a few moments I will be asking you to use your imagination to picture yourself alone in a quiet place of your choice, where Jesus will be joining you. Certainly some find it easier than others to use imagination in such a way, but I invite you to go with it if you can.

For prayer, I think it is always good to find a posture that helps us be both comfortable and alert. If you find it helpful, play some music in the background to provide a sense of being in a different place. Pause to provide the time you need to picture each scene. Do not be limited by what I suggest. If your imagination takes you elsewhere, relax into that. This is an invitation to see more deeply what is already there.

To begin, I invite you to imagine yourself alone in a quiet place . . . This can be inside or outdoors . . . Spend a moment imagining yourself in that place. . . . If you are inside, look around and notice the furniture and pictures on the walls. If you are outside, notice what it's like there. . . . What is the weather like? . . . Is there a breeze? . . . Take a moment to get used to being in your place alone.

Imagine next that you know that Jesus is going to come to that place to be with you. Spend some quiet time now thinking about what you would like to say or do with Jesus. Is there anything you want to thank him for . . . tell him you are sorry for . . . ask his help with . . . say to him?

Now, somehow, Jesus himself is right there with you in your quiet place. You hear Jesus speak your name. Jesus indicates that this time is for the two of you together. Jesus invites you to open your heart to him. Take a minute or two now to do just that.

Imagine now that you have just a little more time with Jesus face-to-face. Is there anything else that you would want to say or do? How do you use these last few moments with Jesus?

Listen now to Jesus tell you, "I want you to know that I understand what it is like for you. And I care for you more than you will ever know."

Jesus then says your name again, looks right at you, and says, "I love you." You can tell that he means it.

Jesus then holds out his arms as if to give you a hug. If you are able, go ahead and let that happen. Bury your face in his chest and let him put his arms around you and hold you for a moment.

As Jesus gently releases you, he looks right at you and smiles. He tells you that he will be with you always. Listen to him promise to always be with you, loving you.

Then Jesus is gone from your sight. In your mind's eye as you look around in your quiet place you no longer see Jesus there. But if you can, let yourself sense his presence still with you there.

Now come back to an awareness of the place you are now. As you do so, know that Jesus is still with you, here and now.

Certainly some find it easier than others to use imagination in prayer. Whether you found this exercise helpful or distracting, it is still the truth that no matter where we go or what situation we find ourselves in, Jesus is already there waiting to catch us in the arms of love.